My Mess Became My Message

By
Shalaunda "Shay" Nielsen

Copyright © 2012 by Shay Nielsen

My Mess Became My Message
by Shay Nielsen

Printed in the United States of America

ISBN 9781624195075

All rights reserved solely by the author. The author guarantees all contents are original and do not infringe upon the legal rights of any other person or work. No part of this book may be reproduced in any form without the permission of the author. The views expressed in this book are not necessarily those of the publisher.

Unless otherwise indicated, Bible quotations are taken from The Good News Translation® (Today's English Version, Second Edition). Copyright © 1992 by American Bible Society. All rights reserved; and The King James Version of the Bible.

www.xulonpress.com

Dedication

I dedicate this book to my Husband, Colter, I am blessed that you met me where I was and loved me for who I was.

> Ephesians 5:32 *"For this cause shall a man leave his father and mother, and shall be joined unto his wife, and they two shall be one flesh."*

From day one you have loved me beyond my flaws and never made me feel inadequate. The life we share together is one that I could not have imagined in my wildest dreams. You have helped me be the woman I am by giving me unconditional love, cheering me on, and having my back. I can say because you saw the best in me, you now have the best of me. As I pen the last words I am excited we have finished the book, I could not have done it without you in front of me! I love you with every breath in my body, from the depths of my soul and for the rest of my life!!!

To my cousin Sherilyn "Sherry" Black, only God knows what would've, could've, and probably should've happen to me had it not been for you. I am forever grateful that you and Yo (Yolanda) have stood by my side. I am humbled by the courage you have shown, the loyalty you have given, and the controversy you have faced on my behalf. I by no means take it for granted how you continually held me down! Thank you, I love you big cousin.

To my grandparents Leslie and Susie Seals, thank you for the infinite acts of love, holding our family together, and covering me in prayer. I am so glad that family is not just determined by blood, because if this had been the case I would not have the privilege of calling you my grandparents. The last name "Seals" may no longer be on my driver's license but it will forever remain in my heart. My love for you is unexplainable and unmeasurable and I thank you for displaying this type of love to me. Rest in sweet peace Gran, we miss you dearly.

To Chance Amante' Seals, you died so I could live. In a weird sense, I thank you for being the catalyst I need to make it to heaven. I won't disappoint God, I won't disappoint myself, and I won't disappoint you. Until we meet again, I love you baby.

To Anthony Chism and Dexter Starr Sr., for filling a void before there was ever one created. I had a father to help pick me up when I fell off my bike and I also had one to guide me through my adolescence. Through you I had men demonstrate to me what type of man I should one day search for myself. You guys may not be able to give me a kidney, but you have willingly given me your hearts. I love you.

To Tiffany Council, Thandi Powell, and Francis Brown, for being women of good character and integrity. At different points in my life I looked to one of you for inspiration, counsel, and most importantly hope. I have never been satisfied with who I was and you guys gave me the faith that I needed to desire more. After all, good change starts with desire. Thank you may never be enough for all the encouragement you ladies have unknowingly added to my life. Sometimes, all we need is someone to show us more than they tell us. I love my three angels, you may never know the extent how of much.

To Bryan Davenport, Chekelia Looney, and the rest of my nieces and nephews, if you can see it, you can be it. Don't be afraid to dream big and

Dedication

never let anyone tell you what you cannot do, because the only thing you cannot do is fail. And if anyone says anything contrary to the above statement, call Aunt Shay and Aunt Shawn will show up! (Insider) You will soon know!!!

I'd also like to give special thanks to my investors; Colter Nielsen, Rodney Sanell, and Brandi-Berry Fulton for your time, talent, treasure, and belief in me- we did it! Lynnette Crawford-Baron Fashion Stylist at Perfect Pink for putting together my entire ensemble for my book release event, fashion is your passion and I'm grateful to reap the benefits of your talent! Contact Lynnette at Letlynnettestyleu@gmail.com for your fashion needs. Tootie Tyler for my fabulous make-up at the book release party, thank you gorgeous! Natalie Copridge, owner of Imani Wedding and Event Productions, for making my first book event a success! Chevalya Barr, Teandra Howard, Anitra McFadden and SaShay Patterson, everything life changing that has happened to me, your faces are tied to the memories, I love you all. To Justin and Rachel Sims, thank you for being an encouragement to me by simply being who you are. You guys are young, beautiful, and after God's heart and you unknowingly inspire me daily. I love you both. A huge thank you to Amanda "Mandy" Runske, owner of Mandy's Photography (mandy.runske@aol.com), for capturing a beautiful photo with less than a 24 hours notice. We shall do business again. And to all my family and friends, whether you touched my life positively or negatively, none of it was by accident and every experience we've shared was worth it: I love and appreciate you all and this entire process has truly humbled me.

Table of Contents

Foreword xi
Introduction xvii
Mama's Girl 21
Church, Church, and More Church 33
My First and Best Friend 40
Angels On Earth 53
Books Before Boys... Wait, Girls? 58
Wedding Bells Or Wedding Hell 70
Sex, Drugs, & Rock And Roll 81
Twenty-Three And Zero 91
Death Comes In Three's 105
My Message 125
A Praying Mama 130
Conviction Not Comfort 134
Married To God And Him 139
Who Stole My Fairytale? 148
What About My Friends? 158
Alter Ego 168
Happy Birthday 172
I Came For Deliverance 182
Victorious 195

Foreword

Ten months of pregnancy never truly prepares you for motherhood but it does allow your heart to love like it has never loved before. Prior to becoming pregnant I think I had the idea that mother's had motherhood figured out from day one (that was an idea that was not long-lived). My idea of parenthood and motherhood in particular was formed by my own life experiences. All before the age of five I had been misused, abused, and adopted. While carrying my first born it was true that I knew little about being a mom, however I knew enough about being a mom to know that my biological mother failed me as a parent. I vowed to myself whether I was the mother of one child or 101 children that I would not fail as a parent.

On December 19, 1981 at 9:33am, ShaLaunda L. Seals entered this world. My first bundle of joy, and this bundle changed my life forever. As I held her and stared into her eyes I said a prayer in which I asked God to equip me with exactly what I needed to be the best mom for ShaLaunda according to her individuality. I asked God for His discernment, guidance, and wisdom so that I could be whatever my daughter needed. Prayer is how I started parenthood and as a parent I have never ceased praying.

I felt like I had already given ShaLaunda a "black eye" from day one by bringing her in this world with just me, a single mom- she did not come home to a "family". Although alone in the natural sense God never left me in the spiritual sense. He was there every step of the way and blessed me to have parents (my adopted parents) and my best friend Karen "Cookie" Hynson. If it takes a village to raise a child they were my village. Times weren't often hard raising ShaLaunda, from the start she was pleasant, loving, and modest. It was her that made me realize my good outweighed my bad. As my baby (whom I now call Pickle) grew older, her seemingly easy-going demeanor carried over into her childhood and adolescence. Pickle and I were like glue and she was not moved or interested in connections or friendships with anyone outside of me. I often worried about her advancing socially because she would not take to people, any type of people, no matter how close they were on the family tree.

ShaLaunda emerged from her shell throughout her childhood as a butterfly emerges from a cocoon. She was always peaceful, kind, and obedient. Obedience is one of her strong qualities and even through her teenage years she never let her hormones change this positive attribute. Academically she soared, was afraid of thunderstorms, the dark, and sucked her thumb openly past her teenage years. Then almost overnight my child changed, it was not gradual but sudden. There was no more, ShaLaunda or Pickle, but now "Shay" had emerged. In complete disbelief I asked myself "where has my remarkable child gone?" I wanted to know where Shay came from and who gave her this name! I raised my children in such a way that nothing in their life should be a surprise to me. I taught my girls that of all the things you might be; good, bad, or in-different; you have to be honest so people around you know what to expect. Welcoming truth seemed as if it bit me in the behind. I was feeling that someone now needed to teach ShaLaunda a happy medium between the necessary truth and tactless, brutal, vulgar truth. I must admit "Shay" had me wishing at times, that I'd rather be surprised.

Conversations with my Pickle, who had now taken on the name

Shay, became the bane of my existence. The life she was living was every mother's nightmare for their daughter's and tormented my peace. Everything from the clothes on her back to the language that proceeded out of her mouth had me ready to grab ShaLaunda by her throat and knock some sense into her. Instead, I welcomed her with love; I did not want my attempt to set her straight push her deeper into the nightmare she was living. One day after ShaLaunda left my home I wept and I wept. It was then I realized I had not equipped my daughter for the spiritual warfare that she was fighting. The devil had a grip on her and that day; Roberta D. Starr confronted him once again. ShaLaunda was oblivious to the attacks of the enemy, but her mother was not. I was well aware of what was taking place and disappointed in myself that I hadn't realized it sooner. I understand what it takes to war in the spirit, and on this day, I put my war clothes on. I began to study, pray and fast like never before. My secular life was almost no more; no concerts, movies or causal anniversary cocktails with my husband. I gave it all up and I gave myself away to be used by the Almighty God. I knew if I wanted victory in this battle, I had to get even stronger in the Lord.

The harder I battled the more she began to sink deeper and deeper into the world. In fact, I began to think my prayers were counter-productive because the more I prayed, the crazier the stories that made up ShaLaunda's everyday life got. I would converse with God and just say "Ok, look, my prayers have been the same in regards to my daughter and nothing is changing, what now?" I knew I was diligent in my prayers yet it seemed like God didn't hear me. I even begun to question if I was praying out of His will and I changed my petition to Him. I remember praying, "Lord prepare me for the grave or jail because that is the only direction ShaLaunda's life is headed. The Holy Spirit checked me quick! I Got back in my war stance and remembered that I don't have children to give away and I owed it to my daughter to fight for her life and her soul, with everything I had. Any real mom knows, when your children are drowning, you don't throw in a life jacket and hope for the best; a mother jumps in- even if she can't swim!

People judged my baby; family, friends, and church members. However at this point the whispers about my baby that once sent me to bed in tears, prompted me to pray for those that dared to judge. We as believers have made this "approved sins list" as if God doesn't hate all sin. Yes my child is doing *this* and yours is doing *that,* but shall we touch and agree and bring them all to Christ? It's a lonely walk loving the child that everyone else deems as unworthy of love, but it was a walk I was more than willing to walk totally alone. I am a real mother and as long as I have breath in my body my children have an open heart that loves them, open ears to hear them, and open arms to run into when the world turns their back on them. I don't tolerate or justify my children's mess, nonetheless they all know they *have* all the mother they need right here in me.

If I could say a few things to mother's that are weary from worrying about their children I'd say this, "You have to be the change you want to see." You can win your baby back, but it's going to cost you everything. You must realize in order for there to be change in your child, the first change may have to take place in you. Love them don't fuss and preach *at* them, you want to appeal to their hearts in love not their ears in anger. The Bible even says that with love and kindness Jesus drew men unto Him; don't attempt to change your child any other way.

Upon reading this book, you should know that once again, ShaLaunda has taken my breath away. This is factual, relevant, and worthy of your time. Only things that have been changed or left out are in an effort to spare the readers graphic details (some of us will appreciate this). When I realized ShaLaunda, whom to date I do not refer to as Shay, was serious

Foreword

about writing this book I directly told her that some things should be taken to your grave. I thought to myself that this child was going to make me relive this again! Shame and embarrassment came over me as she verbally gave me the unedited details of this soon to be book. I told my husband, "Shall we start looking for a new church home, your daughter is writing a book, and surely were getting put out?" "ShaLaunda please give it to us medium and not red hot", I asked with sincerity.

Then, the Holy Spirit reminded me of a scripture, "They overcame him by the blood of the Lamb, and by the word of their testimony" (Revelations 12:11). In that moment, I became proud that my daughter was bold enough to share what God had done for her. I realized in that moment that it wasn't about me or even about ShaLaunda, it's about the goodness of God and what faith and hope in Him will do. Pickle's amazing testimony has names attached to it and keeping it to her self is what the devil wants. The devil does not want anyone to live with hope. Hope gives faith substance and faith motivates God. I stand behind my baby fully as the proud mom that I am watching my baby who was suppose to be defeated, war in the spirit victoriously.

My daughter's life was once a mess, but with God's grace and mercy, He has given us a beautiful message. God Bless!!!

Roberta D. Starr

Introduction

I began thinking about this book very early on in my Christian walk. Going to church every Sunday morning with a heart filled with praise, yet a mouth too shy to verbalize it, I had to get my testimony out. My hope is that my story may possibly save a young girl who might be dealing with some of the same struggles I have overcome. I've learned that sometimes we think there is no means to an end, but the testimony of others gives us hope and it's that small amount of hope we need to get us to the end of our storm.

I've been through a lot in my life; some things people may not believe if they know who I am today, and is that alone not remarkable evidence of God's love, grace, and mercy? As if looking at the sun in the morning is not evidence enough of His grace. I say specifically the sun, but also the moon, the stars, the ocean. Why doesn't the sun melt us, as it could? Why doesn't the ocean overcome us? Who makes it stay right where it is and not flood the earth? And—check this one out—life. Think about it. A sperm and an egg meet in the Fallopian tube, travel to the uterus, and begin to form a human. Nine months later we have the most precious thing given to man and wife: LIFE. Is that not awesome? I don't know about you, but every time I think about how life is created I just want to stop right where I am and praise God.

Man, as smart as we are, could not create such marvelous wonders. My proof of God's love is so minute compared to what we all witness every day, but so that my life won't be in vain I dare not die tomorrow with all this goodness of God in my heart—I will keep writing.

Evidence of God's favor has always been present in my life, though I did not recognize it until later. Our heavenly Father protects us when we don't deserve or even acknowledge it. When I was living in the world, my justification for staying in the world made absolute logic to me. At the worst point of my life, completely overwhelmed by every sinful act you can fathom, I was sure that even God Himself made me an exception to the rule. I was so lost and comfortable in my sin, but by amazing grace I am found. My prayer for this book is that a young girl reading it who has lost all sense of direction will know that if God did it for me, He will do it for you. I hope that one praying mother realizes her prayers are surely not in vain, for it was not my own prayers that kept me here. My mother never stopped praying for me no matter what it looked like. No matter how many horrible things I told her (and I'm sure it went from bad to worse to downright horrible) she kept me covered with her prayers.

I can't thank God enough for my mom. I owe that woman my life because not only did she give me my life here on earth, but because of her living right before me, instilling the love and fear of God in me as a child, in a sense she gave me eternal life in heaven, or at least put me on the right road to get there. As an adult it's up to me to decide my eternal home, so let me tell you where you will find me. I will be where the streets are made of gold and the gates of pearls. We will sing and give King Jesus praises all day long, and no sadness or sorrow will be found there. That's right, heaven is my goal!So as you read this book and realize how my mess really did become my message, I pray that you read with a heart and mind of acceptance not judgment, empathy not sympathy, and conviction not justification; for it was a heavy-burdened heart that led me to Christ. It was a convicted Shay that said, "I know this is wrong and

Introduction

I cannot live like this another day." It is conviction that gets me through those rough days when it feels as if I can't do this or I am tired of that. The Bible says in Job 5:17, "Behold, happy is the man whom God corrects," and I truly count it a blessing that God takes His time to discipline little old me. Conviction is an honor, and I am proud that God has such high expectations of me. Indeed that speaks volumes to my heart.

Mama's Girl

Born and raised in Kansas City, Missouri, I am a classic "mama's girl" and my grandparents' baby. My mom, Roberta D. Seals, got pregnant with me before she married my stepdad, but unlike some girls who are saddened by not knowing their biological fathers, it was the best thing that ever happened to me. I never missed anything because my "father" wasn't around. My sister's dad, my stepdad, was my dad in every sense of the word. The only thing he couldn't do was give me a kidney, and he probably would have gone "John Q" if you told him he couldn't. I never felt like his stepdaughter, and for that I have great respect for him as a father and as a man.

It was just my mom and I when she married my stepdad. Not only did he raise a child he did not have to, but he genuinely loved me and treated me as his own. He never made a difference between my sister and me. My mom tells me stories about how passionate he was as our father, and it amazes me that a man could be so tenderhearted. Where my own dad dropped the ball, he surely picked it up. Because of his protection, I was never harmed as a child and never went without anything I needed. I had more love than my heart could hold and never felt like a reject. His mom, dad, and sister—my grandparents and aunt, who surely had to know that blood didn't make me a member of their family—poured into me just as family should. Weekends, birthdays, holidays, and any other occasions they wanted to spend time with my sister, they never left me behind.

My mom often tells me the story about how she had to tell my grandmother that I wasn't my dad's biological child. By their actions, my mom thought that maybe my dad had told his parents otherwise, and as a woman she owed them the truth. I have the most gratifying laugh every time she tells me that story. With open hearts, they received me. If that had gone differently, I doubt I would be the same person today. It is our childhood that makes us who we are I believe. Where we live for our first eighteen years impacts what kind of adult we will be. We are products of our environments. My life wouldn't have been the same without my grandparents, and I will be forever grateful.

Speaking of family let me tell you about my precious, beautiful, speaks-her-mind baby sister- Delores "Dee-Dee" Chism. I have what seems like hundreds of sisters, but when I say sister singled out like that I am usually talking about my little sister or my God sister, Andrea "Drea" Looney. My God Sister Andrea is my cousin because she is my stepdad's niece, but she is also my God sister because she is my mom's God daughter. She's never been anything less than a sister to me and for most of the crazy events that took place in my life, Drea was there! Dee-Dee is the love of my life and I protected her with my own life. Though we have a big brother who should do that, I felt like no one could do it better than me.

The story behind our older brother, Jason Seals is strange, and I still only halfway understand it, but he never lived with us. Jason was so musically inclined, if he had pursued his passion for music he probably would be Diddy by now taking care of all of us. He is a minister and has been for years now, married with two daughters.

Anyway, all through our childhood I was Dee-Dee's bodyguard. You couldn't touch a hair on her head without having to answer to her big sister. Being only twenty months apart, we are very close. Growing up with my sister was so incredible and unforgettable. Though I was the big sister, I was definitely the scared one and she was fearless, to say the least. I thought every child was a little scared, but no, not my sister. Thunderstorms, I was in bed with her. Scary movies, she already knew it was time to scoot over. The dark, I dare not be caught anywhere near it, but my sister didn't care about any of that. She was so courageous, yet somehow I felt the need to protect her. I didn't even let her take her own spankings from our mom. It would break my heart to see her cry, so before my mom could get her arm back far enough with the belt I had mine in the air saying, "Mama, whoop me, I did it!"—lying my butt off, but I'd rather endure the pain than watch her cry what was probably fake tears (remember she is really the tough one).

You could not give me a piece of candy without me giving my Dee-Dee some. She didn't like any of my friends, and she still is funny about people I bring around because she loves her big sister so much and she doesn't think any of them are deserving. Growing up, she would act like she didn't want stuff if she knew I wanted it just so I would take it. She knew me well enough to know that if there was one piece of anything left, without question it was hers. Say one bad thing about her big sister and you had a fight on your hands. She has a heart as pure as gold, and there wasn't much, if anything at all, that we didn't know about each other. We never got in arguments unless it was about me getting upset because she was mouthing off to our mom.

My sister and I are also very opposite. I was a mild-mannered passive child while she was called the "mouth of the South" for numerous reasons. Her tongue was quicker than lightning so you'd better be careful how you looked at her. Her tongue was so fast that sometimes she would forget who she was talking to. So that was the only time I'd get mad at my baby, and even then I detested it. A lot of things I learned about love, such as being protective, selfless, and forgiving, I learned from loving my baby sister. Besides the bond I shared with my mom, my sister and I are connected as much as any two people can be.

In 1993, when my mom remarried her current husband, my daddy, my sister and I were no longer a duo. Daddy had five children that were added to our bunch, but only three of them moved in with us. Now there is a testimony behind blended families that truly work, but that testimony is for my mom and dad to give so I will just give a short version from my point of view: DRAMA, DRAMA, AND MORE DRAMA! It really can be summed up just that simply - us against them, them against us, with mom and dad always in the middle.

Looking back, I have no idea how my parents made it through it, but one day it was just like something clicked in my mom and dad. Being a married woman myself now, I can tell you exactly what it was. Ephesians 5:31 says, "For this cause shall a man leave his father and mother and be joined with his wife, and they two will become one flesh." I think when they both realized that no one, not even us kids, could come between their union because they were one, it was game over. We soon learned that their love for each other was greater than any petty mess we were fighting about. As they changed, so did everyone involved in the scenario.

Today I can see the difference it made when they started giving everything to God rather than each other and their own flesh. After so long, there was peace in our home again. The fights didn't end with daddy saying he was taking his kids and leaving, or my mom saying we were going to grandma and grandpas. God had moved into our home, and we all soon realized it. Today, we all get along well and our parents are happily married. Now when we talk to each other it's like, that's your mama and that's your daddy. You wouldn't believe half the mess we went through if I told you because we are truly a family now. I tip my hat to my parents for making it—I sure couldn't have done it.

My mother is very strong-willed, independent, and solid. She was very protective of us and cautious about whom she kept in her circle because she was raising girls. She was not the "do what I say not what I do" type of mother. She led by example in everything she did. We grew up and we made a lot of mistakes, but it was not because we had a mom who didn't care or hadn't showed us the way. From cleaning a home and cooking a meal to being a wife and mother one day ourselves, she covered it all from A-Z. She demonstrated and told us everything we needed to know to survive and succeed in life.

We were never allowed to go over to friends' houses like other children did. I thought my mom was nuts. She'd say, "I don't know what happens in someone else's home but I know what happens in mine," or "y'all aren't going over their house and sleeping on the floor; you have beds right here with good mattresses on them." My sister and I thought for sure our mom was out of her mind because most of these friends were our family members. But spending the night at friends' houses was absolutely out of the question, so we dare not even fix our lips to ask. We couldn't eat other people's food if she didn't know what their kitchen looked like on a daily basis, we couldn't sit on anyone's toilet, we couldn't stay at church if she wasn't there, and we couldn't go outside and play before she saw that our homework was complete and accurate. I know that one sounds normal, but most kids in our neighborhood would just open the door, throw their backpacks in the doorway, and go play—and boy were we itching to get there.

My mom went to drop me off at one of my two best friend's houses one Friday after school; I was going to spend the weekend with her. I was so excited this was the first time I was spending the night away from home, outside of family. My friend was the only girl and not only did she have brothers; she had cousins and Uncles'- men everywhere! My mom walked me to the door, asked my friend's mom who all the mighty fine men were walking around, and two seconds later, we were leaving. I shook my head as we arrived to their home because by then I knew my mom's parenting technique well enough to know, I was not staying there.

We seriously thought our mom hated us. Let me continue so you can see the true depths behind my point, I don't have a bad mom. Church was not an option as long as we lived under her roof, even as young adults. We had to go to church. Kids these days have too many choices, and if you let a child make the decision they will make the wrong one every time. It's scary to think of a society that doesn't fear God, and learning about God shouldn't be optional.

Anyway, we were to say "yes ma'am" and "no ma'am" to any and every adult that we didn't refer to as aunt, uncle, or cousin. We couldn't dare sing lyrics to rap songs or booty-dropping music in front of our mom. We never saw men go in and out of our house, only our fathers and step-fathers. We never saw our mom with a boyfriend, and I'm sure she had plenty. When we started dating, we couldn't call boys—they needed to call us and well before 8 p.m. And until the day I moved out of my mother's home we said prayers every night. I remember my mom saying, "Say them louder. Jesus wants to hear you." I used to laugh but I kept praying louder because I too wanted Jesus to hear me.

I always heard my mom and grandparents say "God did this for me" and "God does anything I need Him to do." I didn't really understand, nor did I understand what living in His will was, but I knew I wanted this mystery man to keep my mama and my sister safe so I asked Him too. Sounds like we had it rough, huh? Especially when everyone around us kept saying things like "your mom is crazy...real people don't treat their kids like that" or "she's going to make them grow up to hate her." Let me tell you, the total opposite came true. I love my mom to no end and she is my best friend. I am so grateful to her for rising above the minimum and taking outstanding care of us. I have no emotional scars, no physical scars, and no mental scars from anything that happened to me, and not because I buried it—nothing exists.

I am so proud of my mother for being woman enough to ignore the whispers of others and take care of her business and her daughters. MOM, I LOVE YOU AND I THANK GOD FOR YOU. Now, she wasn't just this strict "do this, this, and this" type of person. We had so much fun with our mom. We used to wake up on Saturday mornings singing, dancing, and cleaning. She'd grab our hand singing songs like "No Pain, No Gain" by Betty Wright, "I've Been Searching" by Glen Jones, and Karen White's "Superwoman," trying to teach us to two-step. Then she had this deep passionate side to her and she'd grab our face and say, "I love you so much, and if anybody ever tries to do anything to you, tell me and I will kill them." I thought for sure my mom was some kind of psycho and I was terrified of her, but not in a bad way. She was the best mom a girl could ask for, and I will give the same thing to my daughter.

We all grew up and went astray (everybody's child did…it's innate), but because my mom trained me in the way I should go, I got back on the right path and I'm BACK. I will see you in heaven, mama! Now I was disciplined, don't get me wrong, but discipline is an act of love. My mom never yelled and cursed at us, never called us by anything but our name. Whereas most women say they don't get along with other women and don't have women friends, I have tons. I pretty much get along with everybody because I am a trustworthy person. I like to believe that I am the first person you want in your corner and the last you want out, causing many people, both men and women, to confide in me. So I have heard heart-rending testimonies from numerous women. Nine out of ten have suffered some kind of abuse when they were just babies, and I'm not just talking infants here. When I was fourteen I was still my mom's baby. The point is they were children and God held someone accountable for them. It breaks my heart every time I hear a sad story of abuse, but it also fills my heart with gratefulness for my own upbringing.

Most of these children are adults in society now, and they are so emotionally scarred they don't know how to love themselves let alone their children or spouse or a friend. Their parents never gave them the love they needed as children, so love is mistaken for things that love simply is not. My mom always said, "Love is an action word that produces action, and I can't hear what your mouth is saying because your actions are screaming at me." That statement, among other famous quotes my mom loved to say, stayed with me my whole life. It is so important to pour love into your children. God trusts us with our babies, and we cannot take that responsibility lightly.

My grandma couldn't bear children. Many people don't know this, but my mom, aunts, and uncles were all adopted by my grandma and grandpa. Mr. and Mrs. Leslie C. Seals were married sixty-four years before my grandma passed away in December 2009. They helped raise all of their grandchildren and loved every moment. If we have learned anything from them, I hope it is how to be God-fearing men and women. Sixty-four years of marriage is not easy to get through I'm certain, but they lived every day with a smile. I'm sure my grandparents had plenty of fights but we never saw it and that to me is an example in itself. They loved and took care of each other and did anything they could for all of us.

Grandma cooked, cleaned, and took care of the home, and Grandpa was a textbook man's man. He was retired from as far back as I can remember, but he took care of the church, his family, and his church family with great pride. My grandpa had a heart to serve and he loved people. They were the epitome of what I call a power couple. They admired each other, put each other first, and stuck by their vows for sixty-four years. Growing up with them, we all knew exactly what marriage is about. So, to all my male cousins, brothers, and uncles reading this, quit taking the coward's way out and do right by that woman and by our grandpa and marry that special young lady.

My grandpa was the pastor of a small church in our community for about thirty years, as long as I've been alive. He was definitely not a part-time Christian nor holier than thou; he just lived his life right according to the Word. My grandma was the first lady and she was always cooking, cleaning, and talking on the phone all while singing old gospel hymns and praying. If she was on the phone, she was talking about God and always picking up her Bible to make sure she was quoting the right scripture. They lived in the same house for fifty-seven years, and most if not all of their grandchildren went to school from there. We all loved going over there and walking to school together. Every time we drive past that house my heart floods with memories.

Being Christian, they made sure they always lived their life right before us, but my grandparents never forced "church" on us. However they did make sure we knew who God was. I think they understood that the general teaching needed to come from our own parents. I thank my grandparents for being a great example to us and helping to give me optimum care. My life would not have been the same without them. My mom came from a bad situation, and who knows what would have happened had my grandpa and grandma not had the hearts they did and taken my mom in. My mom is a woman of true gratitude and appreciation. She allows her life to say thank you to her parents by living right and taking care of her own children as they did her.

In their late years, my mom took full responsibility for them and stopped working to open a daycare (named after my grandma) to ensure that she could properly take care of them. After living in their own home and being independent their entire lives, it was pretty hard for them to sell the house and move to a senior citizen high rise, but they did. My grandma was diagnosed with Alzheimer's and needed more assistance than only my grandpa could give. Shortly after living there, she started to wander off and they had to do something different yet again. They didn't want to go to a nursing home because my grandpa was still self-sufficient and they didn't want to be split up. So my mom turned her basement into a small apartment and takes care of her parents with the help of her siblings.

God assured my mom that this was her assignment, and she does it with honor. I am awed by her dedication to them. My grandma died at my mom's house, and I am humbled to have witnessed such a selfless act of love. My grandpa is currently ninety-four and still going. He is at my mom's and will be until God calls him home as well.

As I stated earlier, I never knew who my real dad was. Honestly, I thought my sister's dad, Anthony Chism, was my real dad until I was about twelve or thirteen years old. When my mom and stepdad divorced she sat me down and told me that my "dad" was not my dad. I didn't believe her so I guess I just sort of blew it off. Shortly thereafter I learned that she was telling the truth and I met this guy who never has earned the title *dad* in my life. Dad? Where has he been? Why would he allow this other guy take care of his daughter? How do you have a child and not care where she is? *Weird* is what I was thinking; I was never hurt or sad. I had a dad who treated me very well and I didn't want or need a replacement. To my heart, he was my daddy and what my mom was saying was a joke.

So I ended up meeting my biological father, and it was the worst mistake of my life. Not because anything tragic happened but because I was fine where I was. This man was a con-artist and even at twelve I had him pegged. The look in his eyes gave me a bad feeling and I didn't like it and I didn't like him. He started stealing my mom's car, money, breaking into our house stealing our piggy bank. Are you kidding me? Who is this joker? I wanted to beat him. Now you are messing with my family, and you are my enemy. Remember, I don't play about my mom or my sister and he was messing with both. So the next six months of our life was a living hell.

This man never made me feel like my daddy did; there was no warmth, no daddy hugs or piggyback rides or "daddy loves you" cheek kisses. So you can take this clown back where you got him and my life will go on as it has. Even his family never accepted me like a family member. They only stared at me as if I was some sort of foreign object. Family, these people were not. I know the feeling that family gives you. And I couldn't help but think *if you people know I exist, why don't any of you try to reach out to me?* If being able to give you a kidney defines family, I will pass; goes back to another one of my mom's famous quotes: blood doesn't make you family. I have lots of family, most that God has given me, and I am grateful for them and you can't tell my heart they aren't my blood family. That mess with my bio was short-lived, thank God. My mom has apologized to me time after time for his ornery behavior, but I've said it once and I will say it again: no harm, no foul, and no love lost or gained. My mom did what any mom should do and that's be truthful and give me a choice. Life is about choices and the only thing we deserve, is to make our own.

So how do I sum up my upbringing? It was beautiful, peaceful, colorful, memorable, and everything else a young girl needed to become a lady. No it wasn't perfect as nothing in life is, but it was perfect for me. I had everything I needed and some of what I wanted and I always knew I was loved.

I've been through a lot in my thirty years of living but it did not start in my home as most would say, so what went wrong? Nothing went wrong; life happened to me just as it will to you, your child, your sister, your brother, your cousin, your friend, your classmate, your enemy. Nothing can stop a young curious mind. It is how we deal with things that make us who we are. I was a rebellious child but I am an obedient adult. Who I was then is nothing like who I am now. I went through so much stuff due to the choices I made, but it all contributed to who I am today. Sometimes I sit and think of some of the things I did and I'm ashamed to God, myself, and my parents. But I wouldn't take it back if I could. I love who I am today and I love all the lessons experience has taught me. Most children rebel at some point in time, so plant a seed while you can. Set an example because one day it all clicks and when it does, your expectations from your child will be a key factor in the end results.

I knew my mom expected greatness from me, and making her proud was and still is a priority for me. But as a young girl growing up in my grandpa's church, I had no idea how far off the rails I was soon about to go.

Church, Church, And More Church

Having a preacher for a grandfather meant we were at church every time the doors opened. Somehow our parents still thought we didn't go to church enough, but when I was a child I would have begged to differ. Bible study, children's choir, children's usher board meetings, Sunday school, morning service, evening service, plays, programs, anniversaries, benefits and fundraisers—if it was at church, we were there. Even if my mom was working late and we were at our grandparents' house, we knew we were still going to church. It seemed my mom only let us go over to people's homes (just to visit of course, never spend the night) if she knew they were going to church.

As surprising as it may sound, I didn't hate going to church because it was all I knew. Not only was it all I knew, it was where all our friends were. Technically, they were our family members, but they were our best buddies and they were also at church, so I was always anxious to get there. Now learning about Christ was not my first priority as a child, but playing with my cousins made going to church more like a trip to the park. We had a ball singing and dancing in church, acting silly with each other. Of course we got our butts beat if we acted out of order, as all children do from time to time, but we were pretty obedient for the most part. Nevertheless, we did learn about Jesus along the way, even if we didn't realize it was happening.

We could quote scriptures and name all the books of the Bible from Genesis to Revelation in order. In our spare time we sang songs of praise as a first choice and not a punishment. As a kid, I didn't fully understand why Jesus was so important that we had to go learn about Him so much, but when you're young you do what you're told.

Our church was a small one, made up of just a few families—my family! Of course there was us, the Seals', and then there was the Verners, the Wright's, the Turrentines, the McFaddens, Starrs, The Johnson's, and others. We all called each other cousins and nobody could tell us we were not! To date, whenever people say they saw a cousin of mine somewhere, I can spend the rest of the day trying to think of who it was—there are too many to count.

Anyhow, in church we had to tell about the lessons in front of the whole church. Thank God everyone was family because as shy as I was, it was so much easier to speak in front of my family rather than strangers. Not only did we have to tell about the lessons, we had to tell if we had done anything wrong in class, be it Bible study or Sunday school. How embarrassing to have to say in front of the entire church that you were the child that couldn't follow directions in church class, but hey it worked. None of us wanted to tell everyone during lesson review that we were knuckleheads, and this was back in the day when parents still spanked their kids.

Paying attention made me listen and listening made me learn. Everything I ever knew about God I learned when I was a child. Now why were we learning this stuff? Some of these basic principles our parents were teaching us at home, so why was the fear of God so important as well? I feared my mom plenty, and trust me back in the '80s that was enough. Our parents knew what they were doing because there comes a time when you move out of your parents' home and you don't have to fear them so much because they can't be with you everywhere you go and see everything you do. You can develop a "don't ask don't tell" kind of relationship with them if you choose; you're an adult now. Still, I know a God who knows and sees all, and a good parent will make sure you understand that someone besides them holds you accountable.

Involved in all this church I heard a lot about the Holy Spirit and witnessed how it made people weep, dance, sing, and lift their hands in total praise. I remember looking at them and thinking *I don't want that to ever happen to me, I don't like to cry*. I even remember thinking they had to be faking it. *If these feelings are so good, why does everyone look so sad?* As a child, who had never cried out of joy, I was a bit perplexed. Then one day sitting in church one of my favorite uncles started singing a song I loved, "I Moved from My Old House." Now I had heard this song a zillion times, but something happened to me this particular time. My eyes flooded with more tears than I could hold back, but I wasn't sad. I felt an overwhelming sense of joy and peace that made me cry!

I realized later that my heart was full of peace and solace to ease my worry. Even as a child God was assuring me that He was there and everything would be alright. This was around the time I met my father, and I was praying for God to protect my mom and sister for me, and this man left a bad taste in my mouth so I did worry. Even though I didn't understand the true power of God, with hope and love, I prayed. I didn't understand the feeling of peace then but I did very shortly into high school when I felt the familiar feeling a few more times when I prayed to God for random things like passing tests and for kids to stop picking on me.

I don't think I really expected God to answer my prayers, but remember it was all I knew. Everywhere I went growing up all the people around me prayed and prayed a lot. By the time I was eighteen, praying was an all-out habit. I would even pray when I was doing things I knew were wrong, but I didn't want anything dangerous to happen so I just prayed anyhow. As I made probably half of the stupid adolescent mistakes I made, I whispered to myself, "God, we know this is dumb, protect us."

My mom was the pastor's daughter, not a seat I would want to have growing up, but it worked out great for her. My mom is a church girl to the fullest. As far back as I can remember, she has had Jesus on the brain and not just at church, but at home behind closed doors—and I mean any and all doors. Her bedroom door, the bathroom door, the car door, my bedroom door, shoot the basement door…my mom never stopped singing about Jesus. She would pick us up from grandma's listening to Shirley Ceaser singing "I Remember Mama." We'd wake up on Saturday mornings singing gospel songs like "Hold Your Peace" by Albertine Walker. I'm sure they got her through a lot of struggles and storms; of course ultimately God did, but you know what I mean. A great gospel song can work wonders when you need it the most.

Not only did she sing it, she shouted it, read it, and prayed it. My mom genuinely loved the Lord. She would shout and cry in front of us "Thank You, Jesus, hallelujah, Lord, You didn't have to do it but You did" quite frequently, and I'd just stare thinking, *I guess that mystery man only likes my mom because he sure does a lot for her.* My mom was never perfect, as none of us are, but she loved the Lord and lived appropriately in front of her girls. She did all she could do as a mother to ensure that we knew God, feared God, and would one day grow up to serve Him for ourselves. I'm sure there was a time when it looked like everything she had taught me was in vain. She's never said this, but there had to have been a time when she thought there was no way possible, "but I'm going to pray anyway…as the songwriter says, *it ain't over until God says it's over*."

From the title of the book, you can tell that to get the message there

Church, Church, And More Church

had to have been a mess. I'm sure you can also tell that my mom and grandparents did everything in their power to keep me from the mess, so what happened? Nothing even remotely traumatic happened to me in my childhood that would cause me to go over the edge as I did. Most of the women I talked to on my journey through life had genuine reasons. Even if some of their reactions seemed melodramatic, it's not for us to judge. We all react to life's predicaments differently. A few of them say they were too sheltered and simply hated their parents for not listening to them. Unfortunately, a vast majority of them have stories of abuse or being molested by someone they trusted. An absentee father or mother is a common reason as well; and I thank God for taking one dad and giving me three.

You will read about the other father figure later, and I assure you that I never felt like the fatherless child, more like the star actress in an old movie called *Three Men and a Little Lady*. Having a mother on drugs is the least common reason I've heard, but in my experience it caused the worst detriment on a few women I know in particular. Feeling like a drug is more important than you? Ouch. As an adult you learn that addiction is a sickness, and in most cases when it gets that bad it's no longer a choice, but explain that to a young girl who wants nothing more than her mommy.

Another one I often hear is moms simply trying to be more like friends rather than moms, for various reasons. Some were too young to be moms themselves, or they were just not ready for the full responsibility of being a mother so being a friend-mom was easier. Understanding the error of this takes being a mature woman yourself, because didn't we all want the "cool mom" until we truly matured and learned the real role of a mother?

Many people say that I was too sheltered, and for awhile there they had me convinced as well, but the older I get the more I beg to differ. My mom was a parent plain and simple. Though it was God first and church before the amusement park, it wasn't church and God only. My mom played with us like any mom should, but we knew when play time was over. Somehow she knew the perfect balance and how to instill it in us because we never tested her; we knew when it was play time and when it wasn't. My point is, for no reason at all I went far from what I was taught as a child and I tested the water, the juice, and the soda pop. I was just one of those kinds of people who didn't deny anything until I tried it once, and your account wasn't good enough for me.

For the years of stress and worry that I put on my mom, I wish I would have saved her the agony and lived vicariously through others, but I was too curious to ever listen. Seemed like the more my parents, aunts, and uncles told me stories of what not to do, the more I wanted them to stop talking so I could go see what my end result would be. I guess the stories adults tell children to deter them only made me more curious, and all children are different. Still, I believe in the scare tactic. I do regret some of the decisions I made that I will have to pay for the rest of my life. I regret some of the decisions that my husband and I will be paying for in the years to come like destroying my credit. I regret some of the things I will have to tell my daughter that I don't want her to do, but I did. The worst thing you can be to a child is a hypocrite. I also regret some things because there are a few people who will never take me seriously because they know who I used to be, and some people really do believe that zebras cannot change their stripes, so for them my testimony means nothing.

I wish I would have listened once or twice, at least about a few things, but I didn't so here we are. I have an amazing husband who has never judged me, and he knows it all (obviously because I dare not write something in a book that my husband has no idea of). I have great friends whom I love dearly, and they listen to me with their hearts because they know I've been there and I'm one person they can talk to who will never judge them. They are far better at their worst than I've been at my best up until this point. So when I say I've been there and done that, I'm probably not just saying it like some people. I stand here today and tell you that there is nothing and no one that God cannot change, and if you are alive and reading this, there is nothing He can't and won't forgive. I am living proof that zebras can change their stripes. Do you know who made that zebra?

My First and Best Friend

If you think you were a shy kid, multiply it by one thousand and you might understand me. In elementary school I had a handful of friends that I am still friends with today. However, I didn't make many friends in my youth because I was too timid and would hardly talk or open up to anyone, not even my peers.

When I entered middle school I met someone who changed my life forever. The Shay we had known for eleven years was about to undergo a severe change. First day of school, we all assembled in the school's auditorium for the usual school-year kickoff speech. I sat in the very back because I was shy and didn't want to walk in front of more people than I had to. Of course I had cousins who went to school with me as well, but I had yet to see them, so in the back I sat. In front of me sat a girl with no manners or home training of any kind—my lucky day.

Here I am minding my own business trying to listen to the program and observe my surroundings, and this girl starts taunting and teasing me for no reason at all. She even went as far as to threaten to want to fight me when the assembly was over. I was so scared I was trembling from the inside out, and I did nothing to deserve this. I had been in one fight prior to this and it was to protect my little sister; if you've ever been a fighter you know what I mean when I say, when you are fighting to protect someone you love, you almost can't lose. Still, I didn't want to fight then and I didn't want to fight now.

I never knew that sitting next to me was someone who was paying attention to the entire incident and had an agenda of her own. I never really looked at the girl sitting next to me because I was so concerned with the girl in front of me, wondering what I was going to do.

When the assembly was over and we entered the hallway of the sixth-grade floor, the girl who had been sitting next to me stayed very close behind me and I stayed behind the girl that had taunted me, thinking *I don't want to fight, but I'm going to have to defend myself right? I can't let this girl sneak-attack me and just demolish me can I?* My male cousins and I play fought constantly so I just told myself, *Act like it's a cousin and fight for your life.* When we stopped and faced each other, I don't remember what the girl said to me exactly, but before I knew it the stranger next to me was kicking this girl's butt, and that's being gentle with my words. It was the craziest event I'd witnessed in my life thus far, never mind that I was only eleven.

The strange girl only threw one punch before the bully was on the ground. In a flash, the strange girl was on top of the bully trying to kill her, or so it seemed from my vantage point. *Am I the cause of this brutal beating? Who is this girl that is fighting for me? Why is she fighting for me?* I had so many thoughts running through my head it was annoying and consuming. The fight was over and now we were all in different parts of the principal's office. They asked me so many questions and my only answer was "I don't know" and it was the truth. I didn't know why the bully wanted to fight me nor did I know the names of either of the two girls fighting. I also didn't know why the girl sitting next to me fought my fight.

We were all suspended for ten days without ever knowing each other's names or a reason for this foolishness. I spent my entire ten-day suspension thinking about this no-named girl that was my superhero. I mean, really, who does that for someone they don't even know? I couldn't help but think about how much trouble she was in with her parents. She was suspended on the first day of school for a fight that wasn't hers, and technically I was to blame.

Finally, the longest ten days of my life were over and I was officially in middle school. I was determined to search high and low to find this girl, but what was I going to say to her? I was too shy. I knew that the least I owed her was a thank you and a hug. My short-lived search for the strange girl came to an end when I realized she was in all my classes except for maybe two. At last, a name for the mystery girl who had consumed my mind for the past week and a half: LaTisha Richardson, born June 19, 1981, exactly six months to the day from my birthday. We became best friends.

LaTisha, who went by Tisha, and I had so much in common it was unbelievable, but we were also completely different. Tisha was more outspoken than I was and stood up for herself. She wasn't scared of anybody or anything, and she would kill you over her family. She was a tomboy and very sure of herself. She knew who she was, who she liked, who she didn't like, and what she wanted. She wore a confidence that I admired so much, being shy and unsure of myself. We became an unbreakable combination, and you never saw one without the other. Hanging around each other so much, we began to adopt each other's personality, or rather I adopted hers. Tisha was an aggressive person and that girl loved to fight like nothing I've never seen. She would play with the boys in school and shadow box with them like she was one of them. It looked amazing. I wondered, *How can a girl with no formal training fight like this?*

One day Tisha was play fighting with me and I did the usual screaming and whining, but this particular day she told me to put my fist up and hit her back. I remember thinking that she had to be nuts and this was a definite setup. But I knew that the person I had grown to know and love would never put me in harm's way and surely wouldn't hurt me herself, so I put my fist in the air and she taught me how to throw a punch. She laughed at the way I put my thumbs out as if I were saying thumbs-up rather than about to jab someone.

Eventually I got it and every day Tisha made sure that my form was still correct. I would punch her as hard as I could and it never seemed to bother her, but after months of practice I finally got an "ouch" out of Tisha. The weird thing is the ouch gave me some sort of rush and I started to aim for an ouch daily. I bit her, scratched her, punched her, pinched her—you would not believe the pain we inflicted on each other. We wore huge purple and black bruises that turned green and blue like best friend badges of honor in some weird sense. What this relationship had turned into was some sort of passive-aggressive wrestling match.

One day, one of our moms saw the bruises and all hell broke loose. "What do you mean your best friend bruised your body like this? Do you know how crazy that sounds? Give me her number!" That was the first time our parents talked, and they both reported that Tisha and I were saying the same thing—we were playing. Yes, the back and forth abuse hurt and hurt bad, but it was fun. She would punch me so hard I would sometimes cry, but not run-home-and-tell-my-mama cry. She was making me tough and I appreciated it; I was tired of being picked on. The next person was going to feel my wrath, thanks to Tisha.

Not long into our sixth-grade year, maybe weeks, our duo became a trio. We met a girl with the most beautiful smile I had ever seen, and that still stands true today. Camille Wilcox, the girl with all the handsome young men in her family, became our best friend and she was the missing link. She had the amazing balance we needed to keep us from play fighting so much. Camille did not play that punching and pinching game, nor did she think it was fun. Tisha would still punch her and run sometimes, and Camille was playful enough to laugh, but we knew not to go there often.

All throughout our middle school years, the three of us were inseparable. I never wanted to miss school because I had to see them, and school was easy for me so I didn't mind going and getting A's with no effort. Our parents began to talk occasionally and were completely cool with us being best buddies. All of us had three moms now; Mama Berta, Mama Donna, and Mama Wilcox, and it was an amazing bond we developed. In eighth grade, Tisha got her first tattoo with all three of our names on it. I wanted to get that same tattoo so bad, but my mom said, "There is nothing to think about, NO." To me, Tisha made the biggest statement to Camille and me, and I knew from that day forward that our friendship was no temporary deal.

My best friend Tisha was a true tomboy. She never wore hairstyles and nails or dresses and heels, that wasn't who she was, or is. She wore button-downs and the heaviest starched jeans I've ever seen. I swear you could stand those jeans up on a table, it was ridiculous. When we were in middle school, we didn't know what gay was, so it was an innocent tomboy character. Tisha and I learned something else that we had in common that was strange to the rest of the world: we were both affectionate. Being on the outside looking in, you would have thought for sure there was more to it. Tisha and I snuggled, cuddled, cried, and wrote letters to each other as much as anyone could and still function in life. Everywhere we went we snuggled up and didn't think twice about it. Everyone in both our families knew how we were, and it was truly harmless so no one thought us strange.

We understood each other without ever saying a word. Her tears or her smiles spoke volumes to me, and most of the time I only asked what was wrong, or right, to confirm my suspicions. When you are as attentive to someone as we were to each other, they never have to utter a word but you know everything. Calling Tisha and me best friends was an understatement; we were soul mates.

In my freshman year of high school my mom and dad moved to south Kansas City, Missouri, which changed the school I would attend. My heart was crushed when I found out that Camille, Tisha, and I wouldn't be attending the same high school. I cried for months. It hurt more knowing that Camille and Tisha would still be in school together; I knew for sure they would forget about me.

To my surprise, Tisha and I remained tighter than ever and our parents made sure we saw each other more than we did before. They knew we were good friends to each other, and real friends only come once or twice in a lifetime. Besides, by this time each set of parents had another kid, her and myself. Being assured that our friendship hadn't suffered, Tisha and I both made new friends in high school and began our journeys. I'm sure it was easier for her than me; I made a flock of enemies before friends and I am still unsure why.

On my first day at the new school and alone again, a group of girls decided to pick on me, not just one girl like in middle school. I learned then that I was an easy target for bullies because if they looked at me I looked down or away with a look that said *please not me*. If they looked at me laughing, I'd give a gullible smile or a wave that also said *please not me*, and kids are cruel. Yet again God gave me a guardian angel, and this time we had the same name. Shalanda Sanders noticed these girls picking on me for no reason, so she too stood up for what was right.

The one thing I had going for myself this time was training from Tisha Richardson. Shortly after school began, this group of girls wanted to fight me, but little did they know I had a bunch of friends now. When the bell rang they were outside my class waiting and wanted to fight. *Do I grab the teacher and tell her to stop this madness?* Everything Tisha taught me ran through my head in a matter of seconds; should I test it out in a real fight now? I walked out of that classroom scared out of my mind, but I was ready for war to happen and it did. We fought and fought and fought and not just me; there had to have been ten of us, us against them. My life would never be the same after this war. Not that I would turn into a bully because I have no respect for bullies and most of them can't fight. Now I wasn't scared to fight, I could fight, and I am naturally a protector, so this was only the beginning.

Anuthatantrum (another-tantrum our high school clique) was formed while we were all on this suspension- we named ourselves after my favorite rap artist, Da Brat's, album. Unknown to me, Tisha was experiencing the same thing and had formed a clique called The Top Notch AKA The Tops, and they were kicking butt in their school too. How strange that my best friend and I were on opposite ends of town going through the exact same thing. We could hardly get back from one suspension before another one popped up. I was glad when high school was over and the drama that came with it. Trust me parents, do not believe everything your child says because who they are with you and who they are with their friends is totally different.

Once high school was over I didn't want to follow rules anymore so I moved out. By this time I had a boyfriend who had stolen my heart and I his. We moved in with his mom for awhile and then finally got our own place. Tisha loved him and they got along great so we all hung out often. Josh was Caucasian, which was right up my alley, so I enjoyed the whispers when we were out. I have no idea why, but one day Josh asked me if I slept with Tisha. From the outward appearance of her, the question was reasonable.

I was a people pleaser back then and liked to impress, "bust heads" was term. If there was something you did once, I had done it twenty times, or so my mouth said. As with most lies or exaggerated stories, the truth may have been lurking somewhere, but whatever it took to sound better than you is what came out of my mouth at the moment. Sometimes I surprised myself with the lies that rolled off my tongue and for the silliest reasons, but on this day push came to shove and I fell. Josh wanted a genuine answer about sleeping with Tisha. I didn't take a second to think about the consequence of this lie when I answered in an instant, "Yes, but of course." As I stated earlier, Tisha and I cuddled and hugged a lot, but it was never anything "funny". Honestly, the thought never entered my mind about women period, especially my best friend, until that day.

The day Josh asked me about being bisexual put a thought in my head that would change the next decade for me. For some reason Josh felt the need to tell Tisha what I had said and she was so upset with me, it felt like my soul died. I remember the day so well. We picked her and her younger brother Vail up from her aunt's house and that Kelly Price song "A Friend of Mine" came on the radio. Tisha was singing loud and just being dramatic, making me feel worse than I already did. That was the first time we argued and I knew then I never wanted that to happen again. We didn't speak for over a week, what seemed like an eternity for us.

When we finally did speak again, she completely forgave me and it was water under the bridge, but I remember feeling so awkward thinking she viewed me as some sort of freak now. I learned something about the bond of real friendship because we got through that without even a bruise.

So we were grown (we thought), on our own, and with very minimal responsibility—let the partying begin! We didn't go to college like most kids do after high school, we were rebels. However, no teenagers should have been making the kind of money we were making at our age. My godfather taught me to pierce at a local tattoo shop and

Tisha put gold fronts in people's teeth at the mall. Let me remind you this was when piercings and gold fronts first hit the scene, and both were very lucrative businesses.

As all teenagers would do with the kind of cash we were making, we blew it. Tisha and I had so much fun, and if you were with us you did too. Now by this time Camille had her own friends and was mature enough not to let us corrupt her. We were all still friends though and that remains the same today. But soon our duo was again a trio with a girl Tisha met named Malena who she assured me wouldn't like me at first, but I would grow on her. I'm thinking, *Who can possibly not like me? I'm the most likable person on the planet.* I answered my own question when I met Malena at Tisha's job shortly after first hearing about her. I have been alive thirty years and I still have never had anyone look at me the way Malena did that day.

Malena wrinkled her forehead, twisted her lip, and stared me up and down very slowly as if something smelled bad when I walked in the room. Even worse is that she never tried to hide her look of disgust; she definitely wanted me to see it. I bit the bullet and attempted to speak to the frown-faced girl. Hey, it was worth a shot because Tisha really liked her. But when I spoke to her it only made Malena frown more. Who would have thought that this crazy girl would become my friend? Yet somehow we all became closer than close, and it was like Tisha and I had known Malena our entire childhood as well.

I soon came to learn that the twisted face frown was just a defense mechanism. Malena was a beautiful girl, Mexican and black with the most gorgeous hair you've ever seen. Most women were jealous of her so she had few female friends. She probably assumed that I would be just another girl who was jealous of her, but she didn't know I thought I was hot stuff too and I liked friends that were cute as well, so we got along great. The tie that bound Malena and me was trust. She trusted very few and I trusted no one except Tisha, Camille, and Shalanda. Well, I trusted everyone until they gave me a reason not to. Unfortunately, most people had given me reasons not to trust them very quickly, and though I wouldn't remove myself from the friendship, I'd revoke my trust and my heart totally from the relationship.

For some reason I trusted Malena and she trusted me. Maybe it was because I had to work so hard to earn her trust, and she radiated a genuine and trustworthy spirit. Now, Malena's mom, Nick, was my idol. She was the toughest woman I knew and would kill anyone over her daughter. Yes, my idol, a pit bull in a skirt. Maybe we were switched at birth because I acted like Nick and Malena acted like my mom. Let another lifelong friendship begin.

At this point in life we were about nineteen years old and had never been to a club; we just drank and partied at home with family and friends. Malena had a fake ID and had been to the clubs a few times already. Tisha and I couldn't wait to get in the clubs so Malena convinced us to use a fake ID. We gave it a shot and lo and behold it worked. At nineteen, the club scene was like a candy store for a five year old. We were hooked. We started going every weekend like clockwork. Soon enough every weekend turned into ladies' night and happy hour. If the clubs were opened, we were there.

Drink after drink we ordered like we knew what we were doing. There were times we drank maybe eight to ten stiff drinks like it was nothing. Explains why we ended up passed out at the bar table or the restroom floor, puking all over ourselves, each other, and everything around us as we were escorted out of the club. I remember waking up so many days with vomit on my clothes, my shoes, even my hair. Oh and driving, yes I did drive that wasted. Looking back, grace and mercy have done more for me than my mind can even fathom. The bars, the clubs, the drinks and friends—nothing else mattered. We lived to buy new outfits and go to the club, and to us life couldn't be any better.

In the early 2000s a popular drug called ecstasy hit the streets. For those who might not know about ecstasy, it's a small pill that packs a huge punch. Ecstasy contains meth, cocaine, and heroin. Being in a pill makes it easier for people to take hard drugs and justify it because it's only a pill; they're not snorting it or shooting it up. Nevertheless, its effects are as bad.

When ecstasy was introduced to the streets, guess where we were—the streets—so that meant us as well. Ecstasy is a high that I just cannot explain. When we took those pills we were awake for two days, couldn't eat for three days or more, had the worst sores in our mouths from getting dry mouth and chewing our jaws and lips apart, and the next few days were terrible. The pill would make you feel like you were flying in a cloud while you were high, but getting it out of your system was awful.

After awhile I found a solution to not feeling crappy for the next seventy-two hours: take a pill every day. Nowadays I hear people talk about getting these pills for $10 apiece, nothing close to what we were paying. When ecstasy first appeared you couldn't get them for any less than $35 a pill. Through my connect we paid $40, but we got to choose which drug dominated the pill. I knew some guys from Johnson County who made them, so if we wanted to be hyper it was cocaine- or a meth-based pill, and for a mellow high a heroin-based pill was great. Now you do the math: most days it was Malena, Tisha, and me, plus we had also become great friends with Malena's cousin, Amber, a college girl whom I would never have guessed would hang out with us. The point is if you were with Tisha and me, you didn't have to pay. Amber didn't hang out every day or every weekend—she had studies and a real future—but the times she did Tisha or I would spend $160 just on pills, totally blowing money.

Starting to take ecstasy every day became a very expensive habit that we could support with ease. The real problem that was stirring up without me realizing it was the need to take ecstasy to feel normal. I didn't ever want to go through the stage of feeling crappy so I depended on pills to keep me feeling good. All the while, I wasn't eating or taking care of my body properly; instead I just pumped it with hard pills. I eventually weaned myself off the pills because the damage was becoming obvious in my face and demeanor. I looked like I hadn't slept in months and I was grumpy most of the time, and I've never been a grouchy person. I checked myself and started to take the pills just on weekends again, but I didn't stop them. When the street life has a hold of you, it's a strong hold.

Tisha had grown up with a girl named KiKi and they were very close. KiKi was a few years younger than us and still in high school, so I didn't meet her for awhile, but I felt like I knew her as much as Tisha spoke of her. When I did finally meet her we clicked so well and were best friends from that day forward. KiKi became the friend that I did all the shameful stuff with that you usually do by yourself or don't tell anybody about. Nothing shocked KiKi. She was as open-minded as I was and would try anything before she denied it. We were birds of a feather. I think Tisha became jealous of our relationship, though she says she wasn't. Tisha and I never spent time alone together anymore because KiKi always came with us and though I didn't mind Tisha was a little bothered.

Eventually Tisha took the back seat and let KiKi and me hang out without her caring. We were starting to become boy crazy anyhow and Tisha was not; she was very perturbed by our lustful desires. So KiKi and I developed an unbreakable bond and did things together that you wouldn't believe.

I loved my friends and would lay down my life for them, and I'm pretty certain they would do the same for me. We shared some of the best times of my life, and hands down the best memories were made with them. I have lots of friends and I get along with the same sex very well, but when I say best friend it holds a completely different value to me. I converse with, laugh with, and cry to many of my friends, but at my worst, when I have done things so deceitful, so hurtful, so selfish that most people wouldn't talk to me another minute, there are a few girls who have forgiven me and loved me without restriction regardless of my flaws.

Over the years friends have come and friends have gone, but because I have been shown what real friendship looks like, it doesn't hurt me because if they were real friends I'd never see their backs. So thank you to Tisha, Camille, and KiKi for setting the bar and loving me even when it hurts because for me, that's when it counts.

 Angels On Earth

Earlier I mentioned that I learned how to do piercings at my godfather's tattoo shop, but let me tell you a little about this extraordinary man I am privileged to call my godfather. Loyal, honest, ambitious, over-achiever, impeccable, focused, attentive, motivating, kindhearted, compassionate, selfless, generous, dependable, strong, passionate, dedicated—there just aren't enough words to describe what an amazing person he is. Regardless of everything we have been through, he has always been there for me and proved himself in ways that normal people aren't capable of.

As I said in the previous chapter, I do have a few lady best friends and that number has grown today. However my godfather, Rodney Sanell, is my best friend before he's my godparent. He is a parental figure so I definitely respect him as such, but he is also my best friend. Many people have misconstrued our relationship for years because our age difference isn't very far apart. No, he's not old enough to be my dad, but he is without a doubt a father figure.

The role of a godparent is to take care of a child upon the death of the child's parents. Since my godfather and I will be in the same nursing home at the same time, he looks out for me while we are still young, and not just me—he helps everyone in his life. Rod is a successful business owner/entrepreneur. By no means was his success handed to him; he worked like a slave to get where he is today and he deserves nothing less than his success. In 1997 Rod received a small inheritance from his grandma and had a choice between buying an old-school Porsche or a huge building where he could start a business and live above to save money. Now how many of us would choose an old building that could "possibly" be a business over a Porsche that we would look fly in driving down the street?

Being the smart business man that he is, Rod purchased the building and started what would grow to be a very lucrative business in the tattoo industry. Two years later, 1999, he decided to expand his business and start yet another tattoo shop in the heart of a premiere location in Kansas City called Westport. While building this shop, Rod did everything from the floor to the ceiling himself; it was a shell before he got a hold of it. It blows my mind to think that someone can be that dedicated and disciplined toward any one thing. He didn't come from money so he was more than willing to work hard for the life that he wanted, which makes no sense to me because he lives so far below his means, but as I explain him to you in more detail you will soon see his heart.

A few years later he decided to expand the business yet again, and in 2002 he opened another shop on the east side of town that he also built with his own hands. Many people in my life have taught me something that made me better whether they knew it or not, and my godfather taught me ambition, perseverance, and initiative, just to name a few. So three shops are up and running and Rod is doing pretty well for himself, yet in 2003 he opens another shop on the west end of town. Who would have thought that tattooing could go so far?

In 2005 Rod bought another shop on the east side and now owns five tattoo shops. All the shops have the same name, and if you are in the greater Kansas City area you have definitely heard of us, FREAKS TATTOO, LLC. I am proud to be a small part of such an amazing empire. We're not just co-workers at Freaks, we are family. I tip my hat to Rod for being such a hard worker and having the discipline it takes to build five successful businesses.

Being a successful business owner means my godfather is doing pretty well for himself. But as hard as he worked for his success, it wasn't for him and him alone. Yes he wanted to be a successful man and wanted to secure his future, but he also wanted those near and dear to him to live prosperous lives. How many people would work that hard and the last thing they were thinking about was self? After you answer that, you tell me why God wouldn't bless Rod.

I remember so many days and nights my godfather would sit down with me and pick my brain to see what I would be great at and love to do so he could help me to build on that. Being that I was so young, I couldn't wrap my mind around anything except partying, so all his hours spent talking to me about securing my future were a total waste, at that time anyway. I was a scatterbrain so for the moment it was the perfect idea, and then I'd wake up and could only focus on whatever club we were going to that night. Rod tried to explain to me over and over that the people I was hanging with didn't have options whereas I did because he was willing and able to back me on any business venture I wanted to pursue. I knew he was serious and wanted to see me succeed more than anything, but I was too wrapped up in the lifestyle I was living and nothing, not even my future, could make me give it up.

Not to mention I had everything I wanted right at my fingertips, so there wasn't a real rush on getting my life together. It was together the way I wanted it to be. I was the envy of all my peers. Anything I wanted I could have because not only was I making a ton of money piercing, but my godfather didn't know how to tell me no, so if I couldn't afford it or if I had given all my money away, I'd just ask him.

Rod did spoil me and I spoiled my friends. He tried not to spoil me though; he wanted me to succeed and not depend on his dime my whole life, I just didn't get it. I was way too young. Many people think it's because he spoils me, or used to spoil me, that I love him so dearly, but it's not. It's because I still have yet to know one person with the kind of loyalty he has. It's because he believed in me when I didn't even know myself enough to believe in myself. He challenged me for the better and paid attention to what I actually liked to do and tried to find me a career/business that I would love to wake up doing for the rest of my life, and he would help me fund it. Rod has sent me to real estate school, Bartending School, taught me to pierce and tattoo, and helped me open my first business. Not only has he never given up on me, but he cared when I didn't, and who will do that for anybody?

The Bible says give and it shall be given unto you, good measure, pressed down, shaken together and running over shall men pour into your bosom. That takes me to my point as to why my godfather is so successful and will never fail. All of his friends and family can call on him to do anything for them, within reason of course. If it's something that is going to save you money, make you money, or simply make you better, such as rehab or college, there is nothing he won't do for us and that means putting himself on the back burner at least 98 percent of the time. A man of his word, he has yet to let me down. God trusts him with that kind of money because he will do what people in his position are supposed to do: help others.

With him and my two fathers in my life as role models, you know my husband is going to be nothing short of amazing—look what they have to measure up to. I love and adore my three dads for setting the bar for any man that chooses to be in my life. It's so important for young girls to feel love from a dad or a male role model so that no joker can tell them they love them and own their hearts without any evidence of love ever being portrayed. Women yearn to be loved by men even as young girls, and without the knowledge of what love is women fall for anything and often the wrong thing. Too many fathers and father figures have dropped the ball over the years, and it's sad to see firsthand the effect it has on young women. Again, my heart is humbled and I will be forever grateful to my fathers for being stand-up men.

Rodney and my step-dad by definition, Dexter Starr Sr., walked me down the aisle when I got married and I felt like a total princess. My daddy is a man of very few words and Rod a man of a lot of words, but ultimately they both have my best interest at heart and their approval of my husband, motivated me to trust him when I had my own uncertainties. Within weeks of my wedding date Rod and I had a talk and he told me that he trusted Colter with me and everything that Rod wanted for my future, my soon-to-be husband could provide. I held back tears as Rod went on to say that he would no longer get the first phone call when situations arose in my life, and for him it was bitter-sweet, but above all he was proud to see my life finally go down the right path; the path he spent countless hours trying to put me on. I cannot explain the greatness that is "Rodney Sanell", or explain why God loved me so He sent him my way, but I can explain that off all things good in my life, Rodney Sanell is one.

Books Before Boys... Wait, Girls?

A curious alarm clock sounds in your family's brains when you turn thirteen that instructs them to tell you, "Books before boys!" It was funny to hear everyone say that everywhere I went seeing as how I yet had no interest in boys. But since I had my first crush at fourteen years of age on Tisha's uncle, I guess they weren't too far ahead after all. My first crush on a woman didn't follow far behind that. What can I say? Puberty attacked me.

In my mind I thought I invented two women being together because it wasn't a behavior I observed anywhere around me, and when I was growing up homosexuality was nothing like it is now. Young girls these days shave their heads and go to prom together with no shame, and parents purchase the tuxedos for their daughters to wear to their first prom. I knew that my mom loved me and she never denied me, but she demanded more from me and I knew that what I was doing was dead wrong. Back in the '90s, if someone was gay, lesbian, or even curious, it was not talked about and surely not bragged about.

Due to my good upbringing I never went anywhere where this type of behavior was okay, and if I saw it in the stores or other places that I went I didn't know what was going on, and my mom raised me not to stare. Actually, writing this book made me search deep into my memory for the first time I ever had a homosexual thought. It was confirmed by my memories that it was when my Josh asked me if Tisha and I had ever messed around—that's the day homosexuality first entered my brain. What was weird is that the feelings weren't toward Tisha, probably because she was too close to home and I didn't want her to think less of me, so naturally my mind never thought of her.

When I was younger I was the kind of person who, when I did things I knew were wrong, I would vanish from the face of the earth. I didn't want people who knew me, loved me, and expected better from me to see me in my mess, if that makes any sense. I have lost the closeness with my entire family that we once shared because I was so far out there I was embarrassed to be around them; and I miss everyone beyond belief. None of us were raised to even think of half the things I've actually done, so I was ashamed. I could not face the lifestyle I had chosen to live and disgrace my parents and grandparents. The drugs alone had taken such a toll on my appearance; I didn't want to face anyone that I knew would be disappointed in me. Anyhow, I believe that's why my mind didn't consider Tisha; she was too connected to my family. Instead, since I had already used Tisha to create a lie to Josh, I used him to live out a lie that was a secret fantasy.

When you are young, sex is just something you do because you think it's the "in thing" to do—especially for a girl. I'm sure there are a few exceptions to the rule, but for the most part it was cool more than it felt good. Even though Jon and I were having sex on a semi-regular basis, I never made it past the point of pain, so pleasing it was not (I don't mean to be vulgar, I do have a point).

On a chat line, called the party line back in the day, I met a girl named Isicis who had a very striking voice that really stood out to me, so I sent her a message and we became buddies. What was I doing on this chat line? I'm sure we all see where this is headed. Isicis and I talked more and more and I realized that she didn't have the same problem I did by any means. She genuinely liked sex and was rather sexual.

I had so many questions and no one to talk to openly about the topic, so I was all gas and no brakes. After conversing with her I was convinced there was something wrong with me. *How can she and I be doing the same thing, yet it irritates me and she loves it?* The way she talked about sex intrigued me, and more than I wanted to sleep with her, I believe I wanted to *be* her. After a few months of talking over the phone to Isicis, I finally told Josh that we'd been talking. To my surprise, he was never upset about it or jealous. He was cool with Isicis and I being friends, and remember he thought I had been with a woman already so he knew this was no typical girl conversation.

Soon enough, Josh and I went to meet with Isicis. Josh said, "When she walks out, if she's ugly we're gonna pull off." We had an unspoken arrangement, and that night I had my first sexual encounter with a woman. I got extremely upset after the whole thing—and not for the reason you are probably thinking. Going in, I knew exactly what was going to happen and I wanted it to happen. I was upset that Isicis got true fulfillment from my boyfriend and I didn't, and never had in the entire year we had been together.

Nonetheless, we all had fun and did it a few more times, but someone was always upset, either Josh or me. I remember thinking, *This is fun, but it sucks to have to argue with Josh for a week afterwards.* However, I finally understood why people actually liked sex. The passion, the caressing, the sensuality...having sex with Isicis was everything that having sex with Josh wasn't, and I was convinced from that day forward that I wasn't meant to be with a man, so you know what I did? I had sex with another guy to make sure it wasn't just Josh; I never intended to rule out men all the way. Sure as the sky is blue, sex was just very uncomfortable to me; even if it didn't hurt, it did not feel good. For me it was a no-brainer: I was not meant to be with a man, I was destined to be with a woman.

So how did I justify with God the fact that I couldn't date men ever again? (Believe it or not, I still feared God.) I had learned from my uncle that the three key elements to a marriages survival are sex, finance, and communication. How could sex be one of the key elements to a healthy relationship and I hated it? The fact that I didn't like it so much made me not want to have it—ever. What that could create was cheating men, and now that I know what I know I can only blame myself. I wasn't willing to have sex sober; it hurt and it took too much energy to fake. If I wasn't high or drunk, it just wasn't happening.

So I prayed and let God know I was serious. I went to see doctors and they gave me the "some women orgasm one way and some another" speech, but it wasn't a good enough answer for me. It didn't resolve the issue. All men would do is continue to cheat on me, or I'd keep inviting women into our bedroom and that was no way to be in a relationship. I thought God understood, to the point of me praying to Him about how this would not, could not work. There was nothing I could do to change my physical body, and leaving men alone was a last resort, so I was justified in choosing to be a lesbian, or so I thought anyway.

At that point in my life I started sleeping with multiple women, and there was not one sexual escapade that I did not enjoy. In the midst of trying to figure out where I belonged, I found out that Tisha and KiKi had decided to date and were now in a very serious relationship. The first thing that came out of my mouth when they told me was, "No offense, KiKi, but Tisha why not me? We've been around each other forever and you've never come on to me." I didn't realize then that it was probably the same reason I didn't come on to her—we were basically like family to each other. We all just laughed it off; they knew me well enough to know not to take it personally.

I came to the conclusion that I wasn't supposed to be with men and started to think about being with women beyond just sex. My brain raced a million miles an hour about the topic, mainly because I knew this would be a disgrace to my family, and socially this lifestyle was not accepted yet. Could I imagine me with another woman in public holding hands and kissing? What would I do about children if this was something I really wanted to pursue? What would my family have to say about this? I had the hardest time making up my mind, but soon enough the last guy I was with on a serious level made up my mind for me.

After Josh I was in another romantic relationship with a guy that ended terribly, filled with drama, and sent me over the edge. I was certain I was done with the male species and began my search for the ideal girlfriend. I didn't know what I liked or why I liked it so I searched myself first. All my bisexual escapades were with very feminine women, but when I thought about dating women that didn't seem to tickle my fancy. If I were going to be gay and date women, I wanted people to know it, and if you saw two feminine women together you'd automatically assume they were friends or related to one another.

Now in the gay world you have studs, the tomboy that takes on the male role so to speak. Then you have what they call femms, the feminine woman of the relationship. I liked the femininity of a woman; studs did nothing for me so naturally I thought I needed to change who I was. I shaved off all my hair and invested in a couple of baggy outfits. Needless to say, that wasn't who I was. It was very uncomfortable and it didn't last beyond two months if that. I thought after that surely being gay wasn't for me because I wanted to look like a woman and I didn't like the boy-looking girls (studs). What's the point?

One day a light bulb came on and I knew exactly what I needed. I wanted people to know that whoever this girl was going to be she was my girlfriend, so I needed a stud, but at home she had to be a 100 percent girl, nothing more or less. The whole "I'm a man trapped in a woman's body" wasn't for me, but I could deal with the tomboy type of girl that still knew she was a woman. I started going out to the gay spots thinking my search was going to be an easy one, but to my surprise most of the studs thought they were in the wrong body. They were doing everything from taping down their boobs and wanting to fight if you touched them to never talking to you again if you mentioned their menstrual cycle. Talk about an identity crisis on steroids! I was so stunned by this I nearly gave up on dating women. Why not date a man if you're going to date a woman that tries to be identical to a man? These women would go so far as to walk around with straps (dildos) on all day and night, for what reason I still don't know, but I have never been so turned off as I was the first time I realized that was the norm.

To my surprise, someone I had secretly slept with a few times would technically be my first real girlfriend, and I say technical because to date we don't acknowledge, discuss, or care that it happened, but the facts remain what they are. Did you guess Tisha Richardson? Because that is exactly who it was. I can't remember how it started, but I do remember that it was the most awkward thing to go through with. I remember our moms telling us not to try it because our friendship was too important and wouldn't be able to survive if any real emotional damage occurred. My mom may have been saying no for other reasons; she didn't want me to date women at all, no matter who it was.

Our moms were right, and Tisha and I knew it and were scared of losing each other as friends. I'm sure we were both hesitant for that reason, but we did it anyway. We made a vow to always be friends regardless of what happened. So we dated and it seemed like the best decision we could have made. The fact that we knew each other so well and had so much in common kept it alive; there was never a dull moment. I was sure we were soul mates and this was meant to be, and I loved the attention we received when we were in public. I craved attention, negative or positive.

Then I met a guy I liked and liked a lot. Uh-oh! Lesbian girls are looked down upon for liking boys, and I had made a decision and had to stick with it or be talked about. Besides that, Tisha was going to hate me if she found out. So I did what I felt was the right thing at the time and tried to get to know him without her ever finding out about it, and if I didn't like him, no harm no foul, she would never know. I learned a valuable lesson the day I thought that women are not nosey as men aren't. My previous boyfriends never checked my two-way (remember those anybody?) or shoeboxes full of love letters, unknown to them. They took my word for what it was, and I had never dealt with any real form of jealousy from either ex-boyfriend them so what was about to happen was foreign to me.

One night while I slept Tisha decided to go through my two-way, and what she found out was that not only did I like this guy, but we were talking about having sex. She was on fire. This wasn't the first time she had caught me in a lie, so she had already lost trust in me, but what she did next was a surprise even to her. She woke me up in a violent rage and skull-dragged me out of her mother's home, calling me everything but a child of God and I knew exactly why. My guilt kept me from defending myself. I thought I lost a best friend that day, and my heart was broken, maybe for the first time ever. Tisha showed up at my mom's house later trying to carve the "best friend" tattoo out of my leg that I did end up getting. She wanted to kill me—I could see it in her face—so I never went outside.

Again I wanted to be done with women, not only because I hurt my best friend so much but because this craziness was too much for me. I didn't understand how you could want to physically hurt someone you love no matter how much they hurt you. Being with women was completely different from being with men, and I didn't like the inability to control your feelings more than anything.

Tisha and I did eventually get over the situation, thanks to her mom, and REDEMPTION! I promised myself that no matter how tempting, I'd never go there with her again. It was not worth losing my friend.

I started going out to the gay clubs quite frequently in search of my dream girl, and to my surprise my search ended relatively quickly. While looking for who would be my ideal girl, I gave my number to everyone that asked for it. How would I know if they were or weren't what I was looking for if I didn't talk to them right? Of course, most if not all of the studs suffered from that identity crisis I spoke of. It was pathetic and I could not, would not settle for it, so my search continued.

One hot summer night we turned into our favorite club's parking lot and there stood this cute-looking girl that caught my eye. I had to have her. Never being the shy type when it came to flirting exclusively, especially with alcohol and drugs in my system, I approached her and sat on her lap while she was conversing with a friend. I looked at her and asked if I gave her my number would she call me, and of course she said yes with the biggest Kool-aid grin on her face. Now I was always known to be a pretty darn cute girl and didn't have a need in the world, so everywhere I went people wanted me and I didn't have to utter a word to them. This girl was different because not only did I have to approach her, but even after I did she still hesitated to call me and wasn't asking me to be her girlfriend in five minutes like everyone else was.

I liked attention, everything I did was to receive attention, but I could not get her as easily as I could everyone else. She had me going. I didn't like the feeling of not being chased, but I loved it. Her name was Camille and I was dead set on the idea that she was the one. Finally, we were an item and yet another side of Shay was birthed.

Before Camille, I was not a jealous person. So when I told Camille that I wasn't jealous and there was absolutely nothing she could do that would arouse a jealous bone in my body, I was serious. Camille, like most women, didn't like someone with such a careless attitude when you're supposed to be in a committed relationship, so what did she do but bring out the very worst in me because to her, if you're not jealous, you don't care. I learned fast that there was good reason why I kept a careless demeanor, and it wasn't because I didn't care. It was because I wanted to keep the peace. I didn't like to argue. I absolutely hated to fight, so I would hide my real feelings to keep everything kosher.

Camille and I began to fight, and at first it wasn't too bad. I kind of liked being in touch with my feelings; I never had been before. Soon I turned into an overly jealous, possessive psycho who never wanted her to leave my sight and would fight her for going to see her family and friends. There was a rage inside of me that I hated about myself, and I despised Camille for bringing this to the surface.

I've done everything from fight Camille in public to pull guns on her in private; I totally lost sight of who I was. I went from a person that never uttered a complaint to a raging lunatic that I myself didn't even like. At this point the only reasoning I had was I was so *in love* with Camille that whether she felt this way or not, death would be all that separated us. I later learned that God put men and women together for a reason and my irrational behavior is more than enough reasoning for me to *never* question His divine order.

When my relationship with Camille ended, I knew in my heart that I was done with women. Being with women brought out the absolute worst in me, and it appeared easier to control my feelings in a relationship with a man who hid his feelings as well, because typically it's harder for men to expose how they feel. That alone was reason enough for me to walk away and never look back. Yes, I liked the sex, but sex was something I could live without if need be, so it wasn't enough to keep me on that side of the fence.

I told my mom, my friends, everyone: no more girls for me. I started hanging out with "old faithful," a guy from my youth whom I would have loved being with back then, but the timing was never right and when it was he had too much drama for me, and that's what I was trying to avoid. Somehow I got blindsided and off track from my boyfriend hunt when Malena called me one day and introduced me to the girl who would be my second serious lesbian partner.

Her name was Melissa and she was absolutely stunning. When they sent me the picture of Melissa, I remember thinking, *This girl is gorgeous, but I am so done with the craziness that comes along with being with women... I don't care how cute she is.* I honestly went into it thinking it would be nothing more than a fling because my taste in women was so specific. Unbeknown to me, Melissa was even more feminine than Camille, but like Camille her outward appearance was contrary to her character. The more I talked and got to know Melissa, the more I realized that not only was she my type, but I could be myself—which was completely psychotic by this point—and she liked it.

Very early into meeting Melissa, she was also conversing with another young lady at the local gay bar we all went to, and I didn't like the competition. Discreetly, I warned her that she needed to dismiss the girl or I would unleash the dragon. One night, we were all hanging out and Melissa ended up saying something disrespectful to me about this other girl. In my mind she was testing me, which was a bad thing to do. I will pass the test (depends on how you view that I guess) every time. I found myself hot with fire, a sign that something bad could happen and fast.

I wound up in front of Melissa's house pounding on the door at 3am. She didn't want the drama to wake her boys, so when Melissa finally opened the door I tried to kill her, literally. I must have punched her in the face about five good times. What happened next surprised even me. I kidnapped the girl from her home and drove around thinking what in the world am I going to do with her? She was all bruised up and upset. I knew when I let her out of the car I'd never hear from her again, and I was probably going to jail. I liked her though so I had to think quick. So I just calmed down and parked the car. I tried to get Melissa to talk to me, and after awhile she did talk. I made her promise not to stop talking to me, and of course she agreed, but I thought she only wanted to get home and was just telling me anything.

Restless, I took her home and hoped that I'd hear from her again soon, though I didn't get my hopes up too high. Not only was it soon that I heard from her, it was the very next evening. Not too long after that, Melissa and I were in a serious relationship. Trust me, I didn't understand it myself, but I was happy I got what I wanted. At first our relationship felt as if it was going down the same road that Camille's and mine did, and it was. Melissa and I fought a lot. The biggest difference is that we were a little older and more mature by this time, and neither of us was interested in partying or hanging out. All Camille and I did was party.

Though the beginning of our relationship seemed as if it was going to spiral out of control, Melissa's maturity and levelheaded character began to override my psychotic behavior and we were good together, for awhile anyway.

When I was with Melissa, she taught me a lot about communication and I commend her for that. Today she is also one of my dear friends, and I am not using the word loosely. I can tell she has a lot of respect and admiration for me, and I hope she knows the feelings are mutual. I give Camille and Frankie all the credit for teaching me about relationships. It may sound weird, but they were the most serious relationships I'd ever had and hands down they taught me the most. Some of the best memories of my life were made with Camille, and I had more fun with her than the average person will ever dream about.

In turn, I grew up with Melissa and I can't thank her enough for showing me how a real woman does it, besides my mom that is. I started to put the responsibility I learned from my parents and godfather into practice with Melissa, and only because she demanded it—and that was exactly what I needed.

Today, no matter what, I can call either of them and not hold back. Be it about my sister or my dog, no judgment, no hard feelings, and no love lost. Priceless!

Wedding Bells or Wedding Hell

Josh and I became friends so fast that after our breakup it didn't feel wrong to start dating shortly afterwards. The fact that we were still close also patched up any wound before one was ever made. Josh and I called a truce, no hard feelings, and we meant it. I felt like I was ready to spread my wings and fly, being that I was sixteen when I started dating Josh and eighteen when we split. I was an adult, and even better than that I was a single adult—party time.

My sister Drea lived in a house on the same block as my mom, so I moved in with her and life was a constant party. The house was always live and in color, meaning people were always there and we were always doing something fun (getting into trouble of some sort). My cousins and their friends would hang there all the time; since they were in a gang I pretty much saw the same guys (my cousins friends) over and over.

One night in comes the guy I had always heard them speak of but had yet to meet. Not that I was concerned about meeting him; none of their other friends seemed to get a second look from me. All I ever heard them say about this guy was that he could fight, never anything else. I remember them telling stories about him fighting two and three men at a time and not only coming out without a scar, they all had evidence of being in a fight with *him*. I assumed this guy was probably 6-foot-4 and solid muscle. When he walked in the house I didn't notice him, but then one of my cousins said his name. We locked eyes and I watched him walk from one room to the next never blinking.

Being that I was a little tough myself, I liked tough people and not just guys. I liked my friends to be able to hold their own as well. I had no idea that a guy with such a reputation would move me so much, but he did. To my surprise, he was around the same height as me (I'm 5-foot-8) and weighed no more than 140 or 150. He was tiny. I seemed to like that even more because it was the element of surprise. Who would think this skinny guy could fight like he could? I don't know if he knew who I was, but he sure didn't take his eyes off me either.

His name was Trouble and I liked that too because his nickname really suited him, unlike some people who give themselves names they could never live up to. He didn't walk around stirring up trouble like some people who can fight do. He definitely wasn't a bully. However, if you brought the drama to him, you'd get Trouble in return, literally.

We hit it off right away and seemed to have a lot in common, but Trouble and I had two problems in trying to see each other. For one, my cousins were haters, telling him he couldn't date me, calling it some kind of gang rule or something. Then we had the most common reason why men don't pursue relationships outside of their kids' mothers: baby mama drama. I told Trouble I could handle my cousins and asked him if he could handle his baby mama? He gave me the most honest answer anyone could give. His reply was, "No, I can't control her. She is crazy and she runs off every girl. The truth is if she does something to you and you bring the drama to her, she will tell me I can't see my son, and if it comes down to you and my son, it's my son every time. I can't and won't ask you or anyone to deal with the drama; it's just the way it is for now."

That is the moment I learned about myself that no matter how brutal

I love truth. Being in a few situations with Josh as well and him giving the same brutal honesty, I knew this was the type of person I had to have. If it was going to be Trouble or another guy, my only must-have characteristic was honesty. I wanted Trouble though, and the fact that he thought a serious relationship with anyone other than with his son's mom was unattainable made me want him that much more. I thought to myself, *I am a passive person by nature; this isn't something I will have to strive to do*. I told Trouble that we could date. I assured him there was nothing she could do that would move me to fight her or argue with her—I could take whatever she had to give. He thought I was crazy, but what would it harm him to try? If I lost my temper with her, he would just leave me alone as he did every woman in the past.

Trouble put my word to the test and we began to date, and as sure as the sky is blue the baby mama drama came and came with thunder. She called me everything but a child of God, threatened me over and over again, sliced my tires more than a few times, called my job with nonsense constantly…it was insane. Neither Josh nor I had or wanted children so this was something else that was new to me, and I didn't like it one bit. However, my words will not return to me void, so I accepted all the torment and never so much as raised my voice at the young lady.

My family and friends couldn't believe I would accept all the drama and give none in return. What everyone didn't understand is that fighting her wouldn't prove anything to her; it would be handing her my man and that was not happening, so I continued to suck it up.

Now what a lot of people didn't understand about Trouble is how he got the girls and the good ones at that. He was a great guy and genuinely had good intentions, just no drive and motivation. Trouble made great conversation and had a sense of humor that could make you smile during the worst of situations. He was the least judgmental person on this planet, which made talking to him effortless, and he gave you a sense of safety that was unexplainable. He was respectful to all he came in contact with and people loved him; he was an easy guy to love. However, Trouble wasn't the guy your mom and dad are happy to see you walk in the door with for Christmas dinner.

Trouble was dedicated to his gang life so to date him meant to date all his friends and share your space, time, car, money, and food with them. Shortly after we started dating, Trouble and I were exclusively dating. Our relationship grew serious fast. In no time we were exchanging "I love you's" and moving in together. We were a match made in heaven. At first I was even okay with the friends being around all the time since partying was my life anyway. However, it grew old quickly.

Trouble and his friends hung out and partied every day of the week, and there's nothing exaggerated about that statement. Our apartment began to smell like marijuana and Old English Beer because of the excessive amount of people smoking and drinking there. I worked a lot, and most of the time I worked ten- and eleven-hour days, so Trouble dropped me off at work in my car and did nothing all day except sleep, drink, smoke, and hang with his friends. He never paid half on a bill, never bought things for the apartment, and never put gas in my car with anything other than the money I gave him every day.

This was the total opposite of the relationship I was in with Josh. Josh and I took care of each other, and if I gave Josh $100, he gave me back $250 if that makes any sense to anyone with street knowledge. Josh and I went half on every single expense we had from food and rent to toiletries and gas. Trouble, completely different relationship, completely different man.

I never complained though it may sound as if I am doing so now. I liked that kind of leverage. The secret power of knowing that I could leave and you would need me for the very toilet paper you use every day was satisfying enough for me to never utter a word. I can't easily describe this feeling, but it was comparable to a power trip without the verbal abuse- today I still don't hang anything over anyone's head. I learned quickly that I could never give anyone this sort of power over me, it was too much of an unspoken authority. Being a power tripper myself (privately; people who know me won't believe that) meant never giving anyone that kind of power over me. In return for my money, I could do whatever I wanted inside the relationship and I expected not to hear anything about it, no matter what it was or who it was for that matter. If I tolerate foolishness in a relationship, you better believe I have an agenda.

Companionship was what I longed for. It's hard for me to open up to a lot of people, so once I do I want you around forever. Unfortunately, that didn't always mean I wanted to be in a committed relationship to have you around, though I did enjoy your company and friendship. So I paid to play MY WAY. And Trouble was doing so much foul stuff himself, that if he did care about anything it was only because it embarrassed him. Which leads me to some very embarrassing things I've done myself that are hard to think about, let alone talk about, but this is the true account of my life so hold on to your seat—it's about to get rough!

I can't say Trouble was ever faithful to me because early in our relationship he told me he slept with his baby mama several times, and I definitely expected that. So even though we were in a "committed relationship" it's impossible for that to work one way. My attitude? If you can't beat 'em, include yourself. At one point Trouble invited a female friend into our bedroom, and just as before with Josh, this encounter was like opening Pandora's Box. After sleeping with Trouble' friend, our relationship took a drastic turn. He started sleeping with so many women I don't want to try to even think of a number. The amazing part of it all is that Trouble told me of every woman himself. He slept with a cousin of mine, and before everyone could tell me I already knew, straight from the horse's mouth.

Trouble and I were one and the same; we could deal with the mistakes, but don't embarrass us. I respected his honesty so much that in some weird sense everything he told me brought me closer to him, though it was a harsh reality. In a sense, the truth healed the pain before it even began to hurt. The cheating had gotten too far out of hand though; this was hardly a romantic relationship between two people anymore. The more women he slept with, the less I slept with him and the more women I slept with. Remember when I was talking about my sexual escapades with women trying to find myself? I was with Trouble during that whole process of self discovery, so I was definitely no angel either. At any rate, the relationship spiraled out of control and did so rather fast.

The way Trouble and I lived our life was no secret to anyone. Everyone knew and everyone talked about me. "Not only does this boy not do anything for you, he's sleeping with who he wants to when he wants to and with no remorse." I heard that often and Trouble knew it because he was always around my family and his gang member friends, and they told him how my parents felt about him and the situation as a whole. I was embarrassed—anybody would have been. Even though I was doing my own stuff too, it wasn't out there for all to know like he was doing.

Trouble and I had a mutual friend named Double Dee who moved to the south part of town close to us. His girlfriend, Diane, was pregnant but after she had her baby we partied like rock stars. The first time I tried cocaine was with them and I didn't like it, partly because I didn't feel anything at all and partly because I didn't like snorting it up my nose. I did like pills though so we all had a lot of fun, too much fun.

I grew close to Diane and she became like a sister to me. We just hung out with Double Dee and Diane more and more often, and I loved it. Diane loved to cook and so we enjoyed going over to their house for dinner a few days a week. We would drink and they'd smoke (I never liked marijuana). It was an awesome friendship between us four.

We all had our different drug preferences and mine was definitely pills, but I tried just about everything with them. From snorting heroin and cocaine to meth and acid, we tried it all, but my drug of choice was pills, period. One of the side effects of Ecstasy pills is an overly active sex drive, another reason I enjoyed it so much. Remember sex was just not my thing.

One night while rolling on Ecstasy and drinking a ton of vodka, we all decided to switch partners right there in front of each other. Fun or not I was very uncomfortable. I felt like I was betraying my friend even though she was right there. I've done a lot of things, but sleeping with my friends' men was not my thing, so this was not enjoyable. I remember just wanting to hug her when it was over, like, why did we do that? But everyone was acting like nothing happened so I dropped it. That mess never happened again, we never talked about it, and that was the beginning and the end of it.

Well, I got past that and life went on. We were all still as tight as before so that helped me. However, I soon discovered that Double Dee had a real drug addiction and was also pretty violent. If he didn't have drugs and didn't have the money to get them, he would beat Diane black and blue and make her prostitute for money to buy drugs. I felt so helpless watching him fight her, and I'd get so mad at Trouble for not stepping in and stopping him. He'd just tell me "that's their business"; I almost wanted to kill Trouble.

I remember driving around in the snow to find a corner to take her to so she could prostitute so Double Dee could get drugs. It was freezing cold and snowing, but Double Dee made her get out of the car and stand on the corner until she made money. Talk about heartbroken. My heart was crushed. I still don't remember how or why I was the one driving to do this foolishness. If Diane truly wanted to get away from Dee she could have, and I had to let that reality stay in my mind. This was her choice as badly as it hurt me.

All this was happening when I was considering dating women, and let me tell you the odds of me staying with Trouble, or any man for that matter, just didn't look good. Neither Trouble, Double Dee, nor any of their friends worked a real job. If Trouble and his friends didn't sell drugs, they lived off of women. They did drugs and drank every day of the week and chased a rap dream that most young men are after. It was getting so old.

Trouble and I had almost no communication, and we got to the point where we weren't having sex anymore. By this time I had started sleeping with multiple women, and he didn't notice or care because he was sleeping with women in our apartment, in our bed, whether I was there or not, so really what was the point. I was done with it and wanted to start searching for my ideal woman. He needed to go. All of a sudden he turned into a faithful boyfriend who didn't want me to leave, and I bought it, so we did the back and forth thing for awhile. Of course, it wasn't long before his true colors began to reveal themselves once again and I was done. I believe Trouble knew I was done, and he did the unthinkable: he asked me to marry him.

Marriage was a word we heard now and then because we were living together out of wedlock and my mom and dad would say "separate or get married." So the fact that Trouble said it wasn't shocking; the fact that he was serious, however, blew me away. He knew that if we did this, everything would have to stop—the drugs, the drinking, the cheating, the threesomes, the friends, all of it. He swore he could do it and I believed him. He had never lied to me about a thing.

I called my mama and told her we were getting married, and she was not thrilled at all. As a matter of fact she said very few words, and when my mom is speechless something is definitely wrong. Nonetheless, I was happy. I got my man and we were going to do this right. I called my Uncle Kevin Verner and told him we needed Christian marriage counseling. He met with us and it went terrible. My uncle listened to all we had to say, and we were both so truthful, I couldn't believe it. My uncle looked me dead in the face and said, "Niece, I love you, but I won't marry y'all, not like this." I knew my uncle was right, but I believed that all we had been doing was over just like that because we wanted it to be.

We thought about what my uncle said as we were living life, trying to prove to everyone that we were different. We thought we had it figured out. One night Trouble said "let's do it next week, on the 23rd," so we went to get a marriage license, went to the courthouse on December 23rd, and got married. I couldn't believe we had done it for real, but we did. No more bull, this was our new start.

My cousin Sherry drove us around that day, and we just chilled and had a few drinks. That night we went back to our apartment, and some of Trouble' friends were there to celebrate with us. I didn't mind; this was definitely grounds for celebration. Trouble got so wasted he passed out pretty early. I followed behind him, not drunk as he was, but ready to call it a night. You won't believe the next words that came from my "husband's" mouth: can we screw one of his friends? She asked him if she could come to bed with us. Now from what he and I agreed to and the new leaf we were supposed to be turning over, I didn't understand why he didn't shut her down before she got the words out of her mouth. Not even twelve hours of marriage and things were back to normal.

I did go through with it, but only because I wanted to know if Trouble really wanted to start our marriage off like this. I believe fully that if you allow people to have their way without complaining, you truly learn what kind of person you are dealing with. This was the first lie Trouble ever told me and I was done; that ended us for sure. I can handle twenty honest mistakes before I will tolerate one lie and if you disagree, pay close attention the next time someone you love wrongs you. The truth heals and lies hurt and I'm too sensitive for the pain of lies. Shortly after this happened I moved out of our apartment—my apartment to begin with—and moved in with my mom. I was so far over Trouble there was nothing he could do or say to save us, and this was after being together over a year and married only hours, though I stayed physically for another two months.

It hurts when you have a high expectation for someone you love and trust, and they disappoint you. Now that's painful, even for my "stone cold" heart. In retrospect, that's probably why it was so easy for me to cheat on people. If people I was in a relationship with always accused me and assumed I was cheating, surely they expected it was coming right? Ergo, there's no feeling of disappointment, which is where the real hurt lies. So if the only expectation I had to live up to was me cheating on you, then how could I ever let you down?

I'm not justifying my wrongs; time has just taught me, me! Part of learning *me* was learning why I did/do things. My expectations for pretty much everyone were low, so if you thought me heartless, there's the reason why. Once I see the careless, selfish side of someone, I know not to let them in my heart, so the reason I can walk away and it looks so easy is because I never let people in who didn't live up to my standard of love. Fortunately my mom, my three dads, and my grandparents (The Seals' and The Kings') set the bar so loving me meant you had some huge shoes to fill. Personally, erasing someone out of my memory takes less than a week, removing them from my heart sits right next to impossible; so I choose to fix the problem before there is one. My idea of "loss prevention". Trouble disappointed me and it hurt genuinely. As crazy as this might sound, I expected him to do what he had always done—be honest. If the best predictor of the future is the past, that expectation wasn't farfetched at all. But I was wrong. So I moved out, I moved on, and that was the end of our two-month marriage.

Today I have no hard feelings towards Trouble. We were young, doing nothing but getting prepared for the people we are today. We lived through it all, and I appreciate learning lessons of all kinds, good and bad ones. Two things are certain about this scenario: I admire honesty and people who cannot only give it but receive it. And I definitely know now how NOT to be married.

Sex, Drugs, & Rock and Roll

The only way I've ever learned anything was the hard way. For me, the statement "no pain, no gain" couldn't be more true. If I didn't feel the effects of a circumstance, good, bad, or indifferent, I couldn't learn the lesson. If it's something awesome, I needed to reap the rewards to understand it, and if it was something that was not so great, I needed to suffer the consequences to not repeat it. I didn't know this when I was a young thunder cat, but I understand it with perfect clarity now.

After my relationship with Trouble ended, I wanted to spread my wings and fly. I had ended two relationships in no time and wanted to feel like a free adult—something I had yet to experience jumping from relationship to relationship. I went directly from being a wife to a serious girlfriend, and it was all too restricted for someone my age.

I mentioned that I was working for my Godfather Rod and piercing at Freaks on Broadway in Kansas City at about nineteen years of age. I made pretty good money and had fun at work. I love piercing, but eventually the partying began to take a toll on my work ethics. The hangovers grew worse and I went from showing up late to not showing up at all. At least three days a week I wasn't at work for one reason or another. It didn't take my godfather long to realize that he had to let me go; I was bad for business. In retrospect, I'm glad he fired me so we could be cool without him feeling like I was disrespecting what he worked so hard to build. I was just irresponsible and careless at that point in my life, I meant Rod no harm. Rod rocks, he justified me because I was young and he has no hard feelings. Nonetheless, my godfather did help me out with money, but it wasn't coming like I was used to it coming so I brainstormed a way to make the same kind of money I was used to making, and with very little responsibility: I was going to be an adult entertainer.

I started doing the house party stuff with a dear friend of mine and another cousin. We were the three amigos and had a ball getting wasted and receiving a bunch of attention more than we actually made money. It was everything I lived for at this time: drinking, dancing, and all eyes on me, and getting paid in the end. Still, I loved money and lots of it, so though this was fun, something different had to happen. I ended up convincing KiKi to come with me to dance at an adult entertainment establishment. It definitely wasn't KiKi's thing, but she too wouldn't dismiss anything until she tried it, and she could be talked into trying just about anything at least once.

Now, my cousin Sherry had already told me that I didn't want to go to a ghetto establishment to dance because those girls were dancing for pennies and attention only, and I wanted some real cash flow. Dancing in the hood in Kansas City is nothing like dancing in the hood in Atlanta. Sherry informed me that because I was tall, skinny, and had a figure that innately attracted more Caucasian men than black, I needed to go to a more diverse club. I knew without argument that was true because all black guys ever told me was that I was too skinny. The only guys who ever really came on to me were Caucasian and Hispanic.

Shortly after having this conversation with Sherry, KiKi and I went to a strip club downtown and attempted to get a job, clueless as to what that actually involved. They actually made us fill out an application and audition. I remember thinking to myself, *There can't be a lot of girls willing to do this...how can they be picky? And an application? What are the requirements? Do we have to take a seduction class or what?* It was new to me and I was intrigued.

When KiKi and I went to the club it was daytime so very few people were there. For some reason I thought that would be the atmosphere every day. Wrong! Another assumption I was wrong about: I thought it was illegal to dance completely nude *anywhere*. I've never been the most moral person on the planet, but buck-naked? This place did say "totally nude" outside, but I thought that was just to get people in the door. No way could this be legal I thought. Not only was being naked legal, it wasn't an option. The manager informed us that we were hired that day and gave us all the adult entertainer rules. One of the rules at this particular club was that you had to be totally nude when you were on stage. My world suddenly opened up to things I never knew existed, never knew possible, and I couldn't believe were happening every day, everywhere.

Both KiKi and I got the job and started dancing immediately. I'm naturally not judgmental and more than I ever turn my nose up to anything, I want to know the why of everything. I'm more of a truth-seeker and figuring out the why, is far more fun than preconceived notions and premature dismissals. So it was no surprise when alternative music, something most people of urban culture write-off too quickly, became my first love. Working in such a diverse environment opened my mind and ears to some of the best music my ears had heard. Even Camille and her friends began to listen to alternative music and to my surprise they actually liked it and would request it in our travels. I love people with open (big) minds- closed mined people are small minded people: How will you ever expand your learning if you only stay in the confines of what you know?

KiKi soon realized dancing wasn't for her and didn't stay more than a couple of days, but I continued to go back because I was having fun and liked the adventure. I loved getting on stage dancing to Marilyn Manson and Disturbed shocking the face of many. I think the hardest part for me was getting on the stage, even though I had fun *rocking out*. I was completely wasted, unknown to anyone else, almost every time I got on the stage for the first six months at least. The alcohol would make me sick and want to pass out if I didn't keep drinking, so I needed another avenue and quick. I was certain of one thing and that was the fact that I could never get on the stage sober. Now what?

The manager started to get on me about nodding off in corners from being too drunk, and I almost puked in the middle of the floor a couple times. After working there awhile, I became cool with almost all the girls and asked their opinion about drinking at work, nudity, and being nervous, in that order. Very few of the girls were sober, and some of the ones that did drink were also using much more than that. While conversing with one of the girls one day, she told me to try some cocaine, but, certain that it would have no effect as it did when I tried it with Trouble and his friends, I declined.

I shared the info with Camille and honestly told her how I felt about it. I liked dancing, loved the money, but could not and would not do it sober. Camille just grinned when I told her of my dilemma, and for the life of me I couldn't figure out why. She thought for sure I had it figured out, her grin that is, but I had no clue of what I was about to find out. Camille and her friends played with their noses as well (what we called snorting cocaine back in the day) and were very familiar with cocaine. Being that I was so comfortable with Camille, I wanted to try it with her and her friends versus Trouble and his friends, who I never really grew comfortable with. I had to know, wanted to know, why everyone around me loved this drug so much. How could I have done the same drug that a roomful of people were doing, yet I was completely sober?

One evening Camille, two of her closest friends Pooh and Charmaine, and I drove to the park on 27th Street in the hood in Kansas City. That night at the park, I finally understood why people snort cocaine. Pooh and Charmaine were so cool and down to earth that I just talked and talked and talked, and they listened.

I still want to know the magic behind drugs that makes it change you completely from being the person you are every day. Somehow cocaine numbs the part of your brain that allows you to feel anything, so talking about the most difficult thing you've ever been through comes with ease. The part of me that always cared what people said and how they felt so much that it stopped me from delivering the truth did not exist when I was high on cocaine. I had known Pooh and Charmaine for only a short time, yet this night at the park there wasn't a part of me I didn't discuss with them. Whatever thought came into my mind came out of my mouth, as usual, but with a detailed explanation behind it. I talked so much that Camille apologized to her friends and everyone, everywhere we went. No matter how much I tried, I couldn't control my need to talk. I was in love with cocaine.

Camille, Pooh, and Charmaine, were as thick as thieves. I eventually stopped hanging out with my own friends so much and started hanging with Camille and her friends most of the time. One of the main reasons was I couldn't tell my friends about my new habit; I knew they would freak. And when I was high on the drug, I didn't want to go out and dance (in the regular clubs) as I had in the past. All cocaine made me want to do was sit down and talk. Even when we went to the club drinking, if we started using cocaine I couldn't dance to another beat, only talk.

I can't tell you how many times Camille had to find me because I would get in a zone talking to someone and lose my train of thought of everything else. She would find me in cars, in bathrooms, sitting on the curb if the weather was nice, or if it wasn't, talking nonstop and the person just nodding and listening. I could not shut up no matter how hard I tried. If I did stop talking to listen to someone else, I'd just tap my foot, bite my lip, and butt in every other word they said. You'd have to talk over me and be good at it or you'd just be listening. Looking back, how lame. But I loved being out of my shell and with no inhibitions. Guess you can see now why I lost my job at Freaks On Broadway. Responsibility became my kryptonite.

My idea did work and I was able to dance comfortably. I didn't have to be at the club until 7 p.m. so the all-night coke binges weren't a problem at all. I'd wake up at 5 p.m., go to the club, and do it all again, four nights a week. Camille had basically moved in with my godfather and me so we had no bills; we just had to support our own habits. Cocaine is an expensive habit, to say the least. Sixty dollars would last the four of us about an hour. One of us would always try to convince the other to go get more. Cocaine makes you fiend pretty bad, and once you start it takes so much will and mental toughness to stop. It's the best high I've ever experienced, but the "comedown" is miserable. If life wasn't a factor and you could survive, people who like cocaine would do it day in and day out seven days a week.

Suddenly I worked to support a cocaine habit, and that didn't seem to bother me a bit at the time. It was what I wanted to do with my money, and I loved being with the people I was with so nothing else mattered. The club I worked at was one of the classiest clubs in the city, so making money was not an issue. Once I got into my own groove I was a heavy hitter in the club. I never left with under three hundred dollars and my best night was over one thousand. I remember one night this Hispanic guy, one of my regulars, gave me five hundred dollars for straddling his lap in the VIP and putting cocaine up his nose and mine with my pinky finger. Once I told him what I had to pay the club out of that amount, he gave me that too. He also let me break off from his stash—enough cocaine for us to get high for about three days—for free.

One night I got so coked out at a dealer's house that after taking one look at me, Camille said I couldn't go home and let my godfather see me in that condition. So we went to a hotel and I slept for two days. I would wake up, watch Camille snorting, and go right back to sleep. I didn't do any coke for a week after that, which is a lot for someone with a habit. I believe it was then that I realized the toll cocaine was taking on my body and everyday functioning in life. I had to get a grip because at the rate I was going I would be broke, nocturnal, and bone skinny. Already slender built, I had no room to lose weight, and at this point I was under 100 pounds. We all learned to control our habit, and cocaine became a weekend thing—and only one day out of the weekend.

During my days of drinking and drugging, there were some times that weren't so fun and were pretty scary. There were nights I know I should have been dead, and the more I look back the more I fall to my knees. One such night Diane and I (she also worked at the club I danced at) went to a hotel with a girl we were friends with and thought was pretty cool. The girl told Diane and me that we were just going to hang out with some friends and possibly dance for them, she wasn't sure. So we get there and were all rolling on Ecstasy when suddenly our friend disappears and it's just Diane and me with about five guys we did not know from Adam.

Diane and I were high out of our minds, and we both instantly got the feeling that something wasn't right. Even on ex we both got a bad vibe almost instantaneously. I could see the fear in her eyes and I'm sure the feelings were mutual. We were sitting on the bed and the guys start rubbing on our backs and unzipping their pants. I grab my friend and tell the guys "we don't know what she told you, but it's not that kind of party." They inform us that she owed them money for *crack* and we were the tradeoff. CRACK, are you kidding me? I think she assumed we were so high on some pretty good pills that we would do whatever, and since she sold her body to these guys for drugs before, certainly two girls would square away her debt. I couldn't believe this; more than I was mad about or scared of the situation, I wanted to kill her for attempting to put us in harm's way because of her crack habit. I was burning with rage but overwhelmed by fear.

Diane and I pleaded with the guys, and they let us leave after telling us that our friend was a crackhead that we needed to stay away from. Thank God these guys weren't willing to rape anyone for any reason— I remember a guy saying that verbatim. That's the last thing they said before they told us we could leave, and they told us to inform our now ex-friend that she would be hearing from them. I was so scared that night I can't believe I didn't have a heart attack. It really didn't look like they were going to let us leave the way they swarmed around us, closing us in from every angle, getting closer and closer.

Tisha came to pick us up, and she was so upset she had to go fight the girl and would not stop until she felt her wrath. By the time Tisha left the girl was so messed up she was unrecognizable to those who knew her most. Guess she realized she messed with the wrong ones because to date I have never seen her again.

Drugs and alcohol had taken me so far out of character that today, whenever people talk about my past, they talk about a Shay I don't know. I hear people say things that I've said and done that in my sober mind I'd never say or do. When I try to tell people, after listening to them describe me, that that is not me, I can't convince them otherwise and I eventually give up. Because of the decisions I've made, there are people who believe I am somebody that I am not—who the drugs made me when I was on them.

If I hadn't discovered cocaine, I wouldn't have danced as long as I did. I know that for sure because my shyness consumed me. If we didn't want to go on stage at the club, we could pay to skip our turn in the rotation so we didn't have to get up there. When I didn't have alcohol or couldn't get a hold of drugs, I'd skip all night because I could not find the courage to go up there. What is it in drugs that can take the person you are every day, or the person you've been your entire life, and totally change it?

When you are using, you don't really think about how what you're doing can have an effect on your body, especially your brain, heart, liver, etc. I'd love to take a look inside my brain and see just how damaged it is from drugs. I make jokes about my memory every day and laugh at the fact that I honestly cannot remember a thing. There are things that are important to me from my childhood twenty years ago or my current life twenty minutes ago that I just can't remember no matter how much effort I put toward trying. I pray often that I don't suffer from Alzheimer's at an early age, but the reality is I just might.

However, I am so grateful that no matter how many drugs I did, I never sold my body or anything else to support my habit. I never stole money from my mom and dad ever, but especially to buy drugs. I've never pawned or sold anything for drugs, and I've never lied to get money for drugs. I've never stood on a corner looking for the drug man in the middle of the night, and I've never fought anyone to support my habit. I did a drug that usually sends people to jail, kills them, or causes them to wind up living on the streets and losing everything, because after so long becoming a functioning user is not an option. Yet I stand here today drug-free and I've never been to a rehab. I've never been a part of a twelve-step program or even so much as talked to a counselor. I used to think my strong will was to thank for my overcoming drugs without a struggle. Boy was I silly!

Twenty-Three and Zero

My best friend Tisha was known as a fighter from the time I met her when we were eleven years old until now. One of the only things Tisha did not like about me was how passive I was and how I let people walk all over me. When Tisha and I became friends, not only did she protect me and chin-check anyone who meant me any harm, she taught me to protect myself so that when she wasn't around, she wouldn't have to worry about me.

Tisha was a protector in every sense of the word, and the thought of someone hurting me or anyone else she loved would send her into a fit of rage. She would stop at nothing until she brought to justice the people who tried to hurt her loved ones. I was the same way; I just hadn't uncovered it as early as Tisha did. She would get so mad when she'd see me crying because someone or something had hurt me, and I did nothing about it but cry to myself. Tisha, you sure opened a can of worms didn't you!

I've always felt like a protector myself, and I'd fight to the death for my baby sister. My sister came home crying one day about some boy picking on her, I'm sure calling her skinny or something close. The fire and rage I felt on the inside was unexplainable; I had to defend my sister regardless of the cost. I'd lay my life down on the line for her without a second thought. The place where this boy got off the bus and where our grandparents lived was about four or five city blocks apart. I never spoke a word to anyone, and all of our cousins were there with us so they all knew about the situation.

I ran from the front of our grandparents' home to this boy's bus door waiting on him to get off. I'm sure the kid thought it was my male cousins who were all racing behind me that he should worry about, but to his surprise it was I. One hundred pounds soaking wet, I stood there waiting for him to get off the bus, and when he did I tried to hit him with a punch would knock him to the day before so he could rethink what he did to my sister.

I remember walking back to grandma and grandpa's house feeling so empowered but never uttering a word. All my cousins were laughing and talking to me, but I learned young that I can't talk through my anger. The more upset I became the less I talked, so as long as I was talking you were okay. The instant I stopped talking, you probably should worry—a fight was in your near future and not an easy one.

As tough as Tisha was, she was no bully. Tisha fought and she fought often, but always to protect someone else, hardly ever her own drama. Tisha taught me without verbally saying so that if you were tough, there's no need to throw your weight around. And don't let people know you are tough because once they do, they will test you and then you will have to fight just because. Tisha was so humble and modest you would never think she was tough. She said "yes ma'am" and "no ma'am" to every adult, and if you said or did anything to upset her, she had the ability to ignore you the first ten times before her blood would ever rise.

I loved the fact that she was a tough person who moved in silence about it. I naturally developed the same kind of demeanor. Being that I was honestly friendly and liked everyone, I never wanted to be a bully. I was bullied often and didn't like the feeling, so I surely would not bring the same torment on anyone else. Tisha and I both believed that when you fight with passion—the kind of passion that comes from seeing someone you love being hurt—you can't lose. If Tisha kept every tooth she's knocked out fighting to protect a loved one, she would be able to donate a mouth full of dentures to someone now!

Knowing how to fight, yet not being a bully, gave me just the confidence I needed to come out of my shell. I didn't like fighting and I felt bad immediately following, but sometimes it had to be done. I have described this feeling to so many people, people who fight as well, and before I can get it out they seem to know exactly what I am talking about and finish my sentence. Before any fight I've ever been in, I'd get scared and not want to fight. I'd try to convince myself over and over again that this didn't have to happen, and I would try to be the peacemaker and defuse the situation if I could. My heart would beat so fast it felt like you could see it through my clothes, even a wool coat. My palms would get so sweaty and my fist would clinch. My hands would shake like I had Parkinson's disease and I could feel my entire body trembling.

I could be wrong, but I think my fear is what drove me to win. Though I was scared, I wasn't afraid to face my fear, another strong quality I possess: courage. But I'd be so scared that I'd protect myself at all costs. Tisha taught me to be an offensive fighter and to never let anyone rush me, but make sure I got them before they got me.

This is nothing I am proud of now, just recalling facts. I learned quickly that if I didn't feel this feeling, I wouldn't have enough strength and power, passion and adrenaline, to win the fight. I could get in my "I'm about to knock somebody out" stance and punch someone in the arm with everything I had and it barely hurt at all. But when that feeling overcame me, I was a force to be reckoned with. That same punch would knock you ten feet away from me. Now that I learned all of that, I had to learn what gave me this feeling and it was not hard to learn.

I say all the time and I will say it until the day I die: loving Dee-Dee taught me how to love. My sister was and still is my heart's contentment. She never asked me to protect her, and she surely didn't teach it to me; it was innate. I loved her in a way that came naturally to me. That being said, the first way to make my blood boil and get me at your front door was my sister. If you so much as looked at her the wrong way, oh yeah, here comes the reinforcement. You could do whatever you wanted to me, just leave my sister alone.

Twenty-three is the number of fights I've been in the last time I counted, and there is nothing exaggerated about that number. What's funny is there are even more after that, but I stick with twenty-three because 1) people don't even believe me when I say twenty-three, and 2) it was Tisha's and my favorite number. My mom often says to me that of all things I was doing in my life, fighting concerned her as much as any of it. She believed that because people knew I could fight someone would stab or shoot me out of fear.

During the time that Camille and I were messing around, we split up for quite a long while—long enough for her to have another girlfriend and me a boyfriend. I thought I was done with women so many times. Anyway, Camille and I split and she dated a beautiful girl who ended up being a good friend of mine, and I dated this guy who I thought was the one. I met Shaun at another club I danced at. We talked, got along great, and continued to see each other from there. It wasn't long before sex was involved, and mix that with the chemistry we shared and I was in love. Shaun never believed a word I said and for me that means "I shouldn't believe you either." He said that everything I said was a joke to him because I was young and didn't know what I wanted. He'd tell me all the time that I was gay and never leaving Camille and that him and I were just having fun, but that didn't stop me from growing feelings for him.

We were never in a relationship verbally, but you know how we women are—I was going to put this man in a relationship whether he knew it or not. One night I went to see Shaun at the studio and then I went to the club, but I told him I wanted to hook up with him after the club. He agreed, and he typically kept his word, so I did my one-two at the club and then called Shaun ready to call it a night. He never answered the phone. I called him probably one hundred times, and every time I heard his voicemail I was filled with more rage than the last time.

I finally left a message that said, "If you don't answer this phone, I'm going to set your car on fire." By this time I had been to his home and his nephews let me in. Shaun's car was at his house, but he wasn't. Furious, KiKi and I headed to the gas station to get the proper accessories. On the way there we listened to some of the hardest rap music I've ever listened to. Killa Tay Mr. Mafioso provoked us the entire ride back to Shaun's house. Listening to something a little more soothing, I might have calmed down. I never thought music was so influential, but on this day I definitely learned that valuable lesson.

As we approached the car, my heart beating faster and faster, I knew that my words couldn't return to me void, so I had to do this or every time I was upset it would be nothing but idle threats. Before I could think too much, I got out of the car and started slicing tires, my heart pounding in my chest. KiKi was with me every step of the way. We poured the necessary fluid on the car, and she hopped in my car and looked back at me like *what are you going to do?* I don't remember what I was trying to do to ignite the fire, but KiKi handed me a twenty-dollar bill and was holding a lighter. I took the bill out of her hand and she lit it.

I had already broken out the window and saturated the car with the flammable substance. With the top down on the car already as I threw it in, KiKi started to drive off. We were scared of an explosion, and I literally jumped in the car and we sped off. Of course after it was all done I felt horrible and paid Shaun more than the car was worth. I wish I could get to the good stuff now because this was so dangerous and could have ended terribly. BUT GOD BUT GOD BUT GOD!

As crazy as the stories in this chapter sound, it's not like I walked around just wanting to fight people, but if you needed to learn a lesson, you'd learn it the day you decided to disrespect me or my loved ones. I'm not a perfect person by any means, so please don't believe I'm claiming that. Obviously I was a mess, but in certain areas of life I was a good-natured person and respect was one of my strong suits. I could and still can innately treat people in a way that the rest of the world will view as being a punk. If they don't speak to me first, I'm not speaking to them. Who is that waving at me? I am not waving at a stranger. Who are you? It's polite of anyone to speak to you and be mannerly.

I didn't care what anyone said about me though; earning respect from everyone I encountered meant more to me than anything, and if I give you my respect, you owe me yours in return, though most people don't live by that code. Don't disrespect me; I can assure you if that is the route you choose, you won't go down that route again. In my opinion, disrespecting someone is like looking right at them and spitting in their face. If that happened, wouldn't we all fight, skilled or not?

Lastly, if you wanted to fight me, you had a fight on your hands. You cannot and will not "call me out" and I not answer. Not only answer, but give you the answer you wanted. What can I say? I people please in more areas than one. Over a handful of the fights I have been in were because of people just wanting to fight me, and I believe they assumed I thought I was tough when I didn't. I was and still am a peacemaker, and anyone who knows me knows this as well.

But sometimes you encounter those people that even calm, polite words won't soothe. You know the kind of people I'm talking about. The more I backed down, the more they wanted to fight. They viewed my behavior as scared rather than peaceful, so what happened? They wanted the noise, and contrary to what they probably assumed, I brought the noise.

For all my moral code about respect, I have to confess there was a time when I was disrespectful to someone and my own rules hit me back hard. It's amazing to me as I look back how life has a way of teaching us things we thought we knew. I am not going to deny being disrespectful to this young lady because what I did was very disrespectful. As a matter of fact, according to my own theory, I should have been beaten up or at least punched. Here's what happened:

My godfather took me to Vegas for my twenty-first birthday and we had a blast. I didn't think traveling with him would be so much fun, but when he's out of town he's not the same person he is when he's home. He's a business owner and a darn good one, so you can only imagine that his life is hectic, and most of the time he's frustrated for one reason or the other, all business related. It was time to let off some steam. We spent a lot of our vacation time in amusement parks (we both love adrenaline) and strip clubs. Because I worked at a strip club, I'd always drag my godfather to them. Guess I just wanted to see how they did things from state to state. He didn't mind going too much; after all he is a man.

So one night we go to this club and it seems legit. The music was good and I had a few drinks, so I was definitely feeling good. We're sitting right around the stage, as close as we could get to the action, and suddenly I hop up and start dancing. Now, in the adult entertainment business, the stage is how the dancer sells herself to the audience. Men/

women see you, and if they like you, when you get off the stage they will buy dances from you, ergo how you make the real money. If someone walks up to you and gives you a big tip when you're on stage that typically means "I want you to come talk to me when you get off the stage." I met all of my big spenders this way. Some men are very bashful and you have to watch for this action.

The girl onstage at the time was a cute girl with long blonde hair, it was beautiful. She noticed my dancing and made her way to my side of the stage, smiling the whole way. Though I kept tipping her, I shouldn't have been dancing—I knew this. They would throw women out of the club I worked at for less. I just wasn't thinking about it. Suddenly the girl whipped her hair over her head and mine so you couldn't see either of us. It's a common move strippers use so I didn't think anything of it. She whispered in my ear, "Don't dance while I'm on stage b&%^$" and head-butted me in the chin. It was so smooth it looked like nothing had happened, even to my godfather who was twelve inches away from me.

The music started to sound like it was so far away; this girl almost knocked me out. I was in such disbelief I didn't know what to say. I don't like scenes and drama, so when Rod asked me what she said, I simply replied, "Oh, she just asked me not to dance while she was on stage." I kept my eyes on that girl the rest of the time we were there, which wasn't much longer. When we got ready to leave, I saw her sitting with a client right by the restroom. I asked Rod to hold my purse and glasses, and I told him I had to go pee.

As soon as I got close to the girl, I wore her butt out. Blonde hair flew all over that chair. I tried to punch my fist through her face. Who did she think I was that she could just head-butt me and I wasn't going to do anything? I'm from Kansas City, girl, DUCK! Before I could blink twice my godfather was behind me and we were pinned against the wall by I don't know how many bouncers and security guards. We both thought we were going to be disposed of and no one would ever find our bodies. I mean, we've all heard about Vegas being run by mobsters, and I just beat the heck out of this stripper in her own house. Surely that wasn't going to fly. Oh but it did. We left totally unharmed, thank God. Rod and I laughed and talked about this forever.

Life will teach you some things, you just have to open your eyes, be honest with yourself, and be willing to say "I made a mistake." Though I blatantly disrespected that dancer, I did not mean to, never had any intention of disrespecting her, and it never crossed my mind at any time. How many people have done something to me and didn't realize what they were doing, yet I thought they deserved a beating? My godfather Rod said something so profound it will stick with me until I die. He said, "We judge ourselves based on our intention, but we judge other people by their actions. We all don't do things alike, and just because someone's outcome may not add up to us, it doesn't mean their heart wasn't in the right place." That's why I fought the stripper. Talk about starting with the man in the mirror! Lesson learned.

I can go on and on about fighting stories, but these are the ones that stick out in my mind to show my true character. Missy Elliott said, "I'm a lover not a fighter, but I will crack your teeth." Yes, Missy, that is both you and me. One thing I can't stand about myself is that it takes so long for me to learn a lesson. I can get a bad result every time I do something but still try the same thing over and over hoping for a different result. Insane? Maybe I was. What would it take for me to stop fighting so much? I am not God. I don't get to decide people's punishment, and I put myself in dangerous situations trying to be a superhero. People are always going to do something to make you mad; surely I couldn't keep fighting forever.

Something had to happen to make me think twice the next time someone "disrespected me." Finally, something did happen and that something was pretty tragic. I can't say for certain so I won't call it a fact, but if this incident wasn't my last fight it was definitely the fight that calmed me down and made me think.

One Easter, Malena, Tisha, Amber, and I were cruising around enjoying the beautiful weather and looking for something to get into. This guy I had been flirting with over the phone said his family was having a get-together and invited me and my friends. With nothing in particular to do, we decided to go over there until we found something else to do. So before we committed to going in, we just kind of drove around the block to check out the scene. In our travels Malena saw a girl she didn't like, and I guess they previously had a confrontation. Malena assured us that this girl needed her butt whooped so we turned around and got out of the car.

The girl must have seen Malena's face and knew something was up because when we walked up to her, her shoes were in her hand. Malena walked directly up to her and said whatever she had to say. Now, we were on the same block where the guy was having the family barbeque but didn't realize it. Malena started fighting the girl and, getting tired of watching, I moved Malena and took over. The girl was wailing on me with her shoes when suddenly I see Tisha fighting some guy. Then POW some guy is fighting me.

Already in a daze, this guy sends me over the edge and I am so stunned I cannot move. Tisha, though fighting the girl with the shoes and the guys, was still able to tell something was wrong with me. I kept trying to keep myself awake and standing. By now I could see the tweety birds floating in my head. I remember Tisha smacking me in my face screaming "Shay, wake up!" as she pushed me to the car, not knowing yet what was really wrong with me. I stagger into the driver side of my dad's car, still too out of it to drive.

Now these guys were all running our way trying to get to us. Yes, *guys*...no women at all. Tisha was fighting them through the car window, punching and kicking. I think they were trying to kill us. Malena, Tisha, and Amber yelled for me to drive off, but for the life of me I could hardly even hear them. Finally, Tisha moves me out of the way and takes off. Not only were they shooting at us at this point, they were throwing everything and the kitchen sink at my dad's car.

Suddenly the windshield cracked and I woke all the way up. As Tisha was trying to get away, she ran into the car in front of and behind us—they had us sandwiched in. We managed to get out of the tight spot and started to head to my mom's house, which was nearby, then decided that was not a good idea. Tisha looked at my face and lost her mind, trembling from head to toe. Everyone in the car was weeping and scared half to death. I think we all were in total shock and disbelief.

We decided to go to my cousins' house where Trouble would be. I don't think we wanted them involved in this, but at the same time we couldn't let them get away with this. When we got to my cousins' house and they saw my face, all hell broke loose. My cousins were like "let's go NOW." Trouble looked at me with the same look in his eyes that Tisha had in hers, hurt and rage. Though he and I had been split up for awhile now, we were still friends. My face looked bad. My lip was almost hanging off my mouth.

We all hopped in our cars, weapons galore, and headed to the scene of the incident. Everyone was hyped, angry, and ready for whatever, but guess what I was doing? If you said scared and praying, you are dead right. These guys were shooting at us, and we were women. What were they going to do when these crazy dudes approached them? Every one of the guys with us could hold their own and yours too if need be. These dudes fought each other to show rank daily. Fighting was nothing to them, and if you wanted to pistol play, they were ready for that as well.

I would not be able to live with myself if someone I loved got hurt, especially because of my drama. I was beat up for sure, but I was alive. I just wanted to go to sleep. It was Easter so my entire family was over at my aunt's house. When my sister saw me and Tisha, Tisha was cool—just bloody knuckles and clothes torn—but Dee-Dee lost it when Malena and Amber walked in without a scar. I mean my sister flipped out. She knew we had been fighting Malena's battle. My cousins had to keep her away. But regardless what happened, we never blamed Malena. She couldn't make me do anything I didn't want to do.

When we arrived at the house where it all took place, no one was there but some women and children. Trouble walked right in the house and opened every door looking for any trace of any man. At this point, their front porch was thick with all of us. One of the ladies said, "There's no one here except us and the kids." Trouble replied, "Okay, and yall gonna start coming up dead if you don't get those n&%%$# down here now."

The lady got on the phone crying and terrified, and we all grabbed Trouble like *okay calm down*, but he was ticked. Everything after that is a blur, but it was a terrible situation. After that infamous day, Tisha and I couldn't work because people were coming to our jobs. We were popular and everyone knew where we worked. Not only that, our jobs were open to the public, and we both had a few incidents at work and had to leave early. We only worked for two days after this took place. It was unreal. We couldn't stay at our homes, couldn't go to work—suddenly we were in hiding.

We thought we were being paranoid until one day at the hotel we heard footsteps and someone throwing something at our window like they wanted us to open the door. We turned off the lights and hid in absolute silence, doing what? PRAYING! I called on the name of Jesus fifty times not realizing His power. There are a few times I've been scared for my life, and this by far takes first place.

As we hid behind the bed, me crying profusely, we hear people knocking on every door at the hotel. Then we hear someone say "I know they're in here, that's their car." This went on for about ten minutes, and it felt like an eternity. My whole body was doused in sweat, and Tisha kept saying she wouldn't let anything happen to me. Tisha was scared, I know she was, but she never let me see it because she didn't want to scare me more. Talk about a best friend. She sat in front of me with her arms covering me saying without saying "I will die for you." No one will ever be able to tell me anything about Tisha. No, she's not perfect, none of us are, but she wholeheartedly loves me and I will never question that. And, as scared as I was that night, I felt safe in her arms; that was so powerful to me.

We lived through that night, and never was I so excited just to smell the air as I was the next morning. The sad thing was we knew we couldn't stay in Kansas City a day longer; things had finally gone too far. We told my godfather, my mom, and Tisha's mom what happened the previous night. I think everyone realized that had another hotel guest not called the front desk, which made security come to our floor, we would not have escaped with our lives. Rod instantly bought us some tickets to go live with my stepmom and dad in Florida. Thank God they were willing to let us both come because we didn't have any other options. Had they said no, I don't know what we would have done. I am forever grateful.

Our lives changed drastically because of one fight for no reason. See the difference in fighting with purpose versus fighting for pettiness? Neither is right, but in my experience one way doesn't come with all the drama. Of course I could always work for my godfather if I came back to

Kansas City, but Tisha lost her job and she made more money than I did.

This was the event that changed my life forever. Suddenly people could do the same disrespectful things and I'd walk away with no thought of correcting them ever entering my mind. We only stayed in Florida for a couple of months; we thought we were grown and my stepmom wasn't having it, so we had to come back to Kansas City. As I look back, I'd like to apologize to her and my dad for being so unruly and disruptive to their peaceful home. Tisha and I should have been more appreciative, but we were young, and though that sounds like an excuse, it's the truth. Please forgive us.

Nonetheless, when we moved back to KC, nothing was the same. Our lives as we had known them changed drastically. Guess the situation forced us to grow up whether we were ready to or not. We didn't go out nearly as much and especially to straight clubs where men would be, not knowing who was who. This was the first time I'd ever been physically hurt from a fight, and I don't care if it was guys and wedges that caused the damage, it wasn't a chance I was willing to take again. I'd like to think that I was sort of cute and I wouldn't risk my looks, as vain as that sounds.

Watching something escalate so far from an incident we had caused affected both Tisha and me in a positive way. We often conversed about the "could have, would have, and should haves," and though these things didn't happen, they easily could have happened. We wouldn't have been able to live with ourselves if anything serious happened to anyone involved. From that day forward I chose my battles wisely, and to my surprise they were few and far between.

Death Comes In Threes

I used to wonder *where do people come up with "famous" quotes? Most of them don't make sense*—until life teaches you the lesson behind the quote, that is, and you say silently to yourself, *oh, that's what they meant!* One such quote is "death comes in threes." It sounds so pessimistic, and I could not stand when my grandma used to say it. To me, it makes people think that when one person dies, two more are sure to follow, and since we will never know who, it can make you live in a state of paranoia. Especially when the other ten sayings Grandma used to quote have already proven to be true, it would naturally scare anybody.

I was a very sensitive child, and I never had much of a sense of humor so I took everything seriously; this was just a saying I did not like to hear. The simple thought of my sister, mom, or dad dying could make me cry as if they had actually died.

My childhood was an easygoing one so I didn't suffer any pain other than the pain of discipline, which only hurts until you sit down and think *I did deserve that*. As you grow older you realize that your parents loved you enough to tell you what was right and put you on the right path. So in reality I didn't suffer any hurt from my childhood. I have no ill feelings toward my mom or dad for anything that was or wasn't done to me or for me when I was growing up. I had everything I needed or wanted and my home was always homey and filled with lots of love; everyone wanted to come over to our house, as crazy as they say my mom was.

My adolescence was filled with lots of drama and chaos, but did any of it hurt my feelings? No! No hurt feelings, and if I was "hurt" it was all on the surface, a headache more than a heartache. I didn't put my heart into anything because I just did not know how, though at the time I thought I was giving my all, mind, heart, and soul. I loved people—don't think I didn't—but I can love with my mind and never my heart. I loved my friends with my heart. I loved my family with my heart. But for some strange reason significant others just couldn't get to that spot. I loved my partners like a friend, but romance and intimacy is an area of love that was foreign.So my point is, when all these dating relationships ended, I couldn't care less, no matter how long we were together or how many times I told you I loved you and didn't want you to go. I didn't want my friend to go. I didn't want the closest thing to me to leave, so you could just take the "romance" out and leave my friend here and I would be okay with that, if I'm making any sense at all. This is why when the relationships were over there was nothing for me to mourn besides the loss of my best friend. I've never been broken up with either; every breakup was my decision. Maybe if it were the other way around I would have felt differently.

Josh and I were so cool immediately after we split up; people never believe me, but my family knew. We got along better as friends anyway. We both liked too much attention from the opposite sex for a boyfriend or girlfriend to understand. Though neither of us was jealous, it's still hard to understand when you are supposed to be "the one" and your mate needs so much more attention than you can give. Friends we were, and it was the best thing ever, no pain at all. I definitely felt no pain when Trouble and I split. The embarrassment I lived with every day while we were together was painful enough. Saving face was worth missing him, and I never missed him romantically either. I was in a relationship with Trouble and his whole entourage, so should I be sad and missing all of them? That makes no sense. We split and the next day Tisha and I were in a "relationship." No pain from that breakup either.

When Camille and I split up, Melissa and I as well, I missed them more than I ever thought I would, but hurt? No. With Camille there was too much drama. I don't like drama so I removed an ongoing problem, and I was fine with that. We also remained friends so I didn't lose my friend—nothing to be sad about. With Melissa, I lost too much of *me* trying to please her, and I would give her up and my right arm to have me back. Never lose yourself trying to please someone else; it's a road to misery and I was there. And with both Camille and Melissa, too much responsibility was on me, and the weight that was lifted when we broke up gave me a sigh of relief. Though I volunteered everything I did with both of them, you don't allow someone to take all or most of the burdens in any relationship. Guess that's the reason I never let people take care of me.

I did suffer the loss of an aunt when I was about fifteen or sixteen years old, and that was pretty heart-wrenching, as death is for any child. It was so unexpected, but I guess that's how death is most of the time. Until the funeral, I was in a state of total disbelief. It just seemed like one day I was at home and so was she, and the next day she was gone. Our mom assured us that our aunt's passing was all a part of God's plan and told us not to be sad because we all want God's will for our lives no matter what that is. We had been to enough Sunday school to understand what she was saying, and in a sense we found solace in knowing that our aunt was in heaven. Still, it just didn't seem real until we walked into the church at her funeral and saw her body lying there lifeless.

My aunt, Grace Verner, didn't look like the aunt I had known my entire life, and it shattered my heart to see her this way. As the funeral went on and we walked to the front to see her, it seemed as if I lost my breath with every step I took closer to her casket. The music the choir sang made me cry profusely; the lyrics hit me in the heart like music had never done before. I wanted the music to stop, and that's not typical for me. Her death ended up being something that hurts as missing anyone does, but because she lived in God's will there wasn't anything to be mournfully sad about. For awhile church was hard and activities were never the same—our aunt was a ton of fun. But knowing she was where we all wanted to be one day gave us a sense of relief. My aunt was safe, and no one and nothing was hurting her, and that I could live with.

When Camille and I were together, she knew all about Josh and me from top to bottom. Camille knew that Josh and I had split up and never looked back. We were now just the best of friends. Camille was okay with the idea of Josh and me being friends, but when it was in her face she couldn't tolerate it. The first year we were together Josh was only a story to Camille because he was in jail so he was never around, only a phone call here and there. Camille was a very jealous, possessive person, but the extent of it was unknown even to me.

Once Josh was released from jail, he and I started to converse on a semi-regular basis. I missed him beyond belief; he had been a major part of my life for a long time and I always felt like something was missing. Was it hard for Camille to know that her girlfriend missed her ex-boyfriend? Certainly so. Had Camille listened to me, she would have known the truth and freed herself from the mental torment. Some people are in our lives for a reason and a season, and the season of dating for Josh and me was over and done with, long before Camille.

One night Josh called us and asked us to go out bowling with him. I wanted to go, but because we were home sober Camille got mad that I was on the phone with him so we ended the call and that was it. Remember I keep my feelings to myself, so though Camille couldn't tell I was heated. Josh called us from the bowling alley again, sounding like he didn't want to go in, and asked us if we wanted to do something else, but we declined. The next morning came and Camille and I were cool.

I woke up to my phone ringing nonstop; it was my good friend Andrea, not my sister. Andrea was crying so hard she couldn't speak. I asked her to calm down and talk to me, never imagining what she was going to say next. She said, "Shay, you don't know do you?" I guess she could hear the confusion in my voice. I'm thinking, *well, no I don't know why you're crying, and it's 10 a.m. so I don't know much of anything.* Back in the day 10 a.m. to me was like 6 a.m. to the rest of the world, and I required ten to twelve hours of sleep daily.

Andrea calmed herself enough to say, "Shay, Josh got shot at the bowling alley last night and he's dead." My mind went blank. I fell to the floor and cried; I could not believe what Andrea just said. Sure enough, her call was just the first of many, confirming the tragedy. I suddenly felt like my world had stopped and nothing was real anymore. I was in shock. I blamed myself and Camille because had we gone somewhere with him or let him come over like he wanted to do, he'd still be alive. I blamed Camille until I saw the hurt in her eyes and realized she blamed herself. I never believed in kicking someone while they were down, and if you love someone you know exactly how they feel without them having to tell you.

The last time I saw Josh was a week or so before his untimely death. Camille had gone to her grandma's, and I told him and the girl he was dating to come by because I missed him. Every time Camille wasn't around we saw each other, but it was no funny stuff. We were done with even so much as the idea of ever dating again.

The next week leading up to his funeral was the hardest week of my life up till that point, and it was about to get worse. I learned the value of friends and family being there when you need them because everyone supported me. My family loved Josh. My mom and sister were also torn by his death; they had grown to love Josh. Tisha and Josh had become so close I'd call one or the other and they were hanging out. My friends, my godfather, and even Camille all pulled through to make sure I had whatever I needed, when I needed it. Suddenly I had a round-the-clock bodyguard and I needed it. Everyone knew how much Josh meant to me.

One night Tisha drove me around as I drank so much Belvedere (vodka) I couldn't believe I didn't end up in the hospital. Every time Tisha turned the corner, I tried to jump out of the car, a moving vehicle. I was so depressed I wanted to die because the pain was unbearable. For once I was actually hurt and I couldn't take it. I would have given anything to make the pain go away. *Is this how people feel when they say they are heartbroken?* Surely losing a boyfriend or girlfriend could not compare to what I was feeling. I started to feel bad for everyone who said I hurt them because up until that point I didn't know pain—I didn't understand it.

There was no justifying Josh's death as we did my aunt's. Josh was young and there was nothing to celebrate here, so my pain knew no end. No answer or piece of advice anyone had to offer made it any easier. "Think about the good times" really made me break down. Things like "he is in heaven with the angels now" puzzled me. Was that a fact? Why does everyone say that when it's not always true? How can they be so sure? Certain things have to happen to assure your place in heaven, and Josh never told me that he accepted Christ as his Lord and Savior, so maybe he was in heaven and maybe not. But the could and could not didn't give me peace of mind.

The facts of Josh's death hurt me even more. For once in my life, the truth did not make me feel better. I didn't want to look in mirrors, listen to music, eat, watch TV; seems like all I did was cry and drink. One of my best friends had been taken from me and I couldn't live with or face the pain. That was only the beginning.

At the funeral, things became brutally real. Josh was his parents' only child, and the mere thought of their hearts' pain brought me to my knees in agony. When I saw their faces at the funeral, before I even looked at Josh's body, I wanted to die. I was so weak I could hardly stand. I couldn't catch my breath, my knees buckled, and it suddenly felt like a golf ball was in my throat and hurt terribly. Not only did it hurt, I couldn't breathe past it. It felt like my soul was about to leave my body, and I may not know what that means fully, but I was slipping away.

With my mom and dad by my side, I proceeded to the front to view Josh's body for the last time, every step becoming harder and harder to take. I finally get to his casket and look down at his still dead body. I almost collapsed in Josh's dad's arms as I reached out to hug him. I trembled from my head to my feet, not understanding why someone took my friend from me, their son from them, and a good friend from so many. My heart was filled with anger, hate, and pain and I wanted to kill somebody.

Not fully understanding the heart of a mother as I do now, I have to say that his mom's strength was nothing shy of amazing. She wept quietly as she stood right next to her son's body and shook everyone's hands as they paid their respects to her son. WOW! His mom and dad both did as well as they could under the circumstances, but the pain I knew they were suffering made me break ten times more.

Josh's childhood best friend, Chris, was also crushed, as all of us were. Chris and Josh had a special bond, and if you knew one you knew them both. Josh didn't have many friends and the friends he did have were through Chris for sure. Josh and Chris were best friends but they were more like brothers. I learned how tight they were while Josh and I were living together. I met Josh while he was with Chris as a matter of fact, and I believe I saw Chris every day of my life after that as well. Not only did I get a boyfriend in Josh, I got a new brother in Chris. He used to call me Chay Chay, and I loved that he gave me a nickname. The thought of what Chris was suffering right now made this whole ordeal that much more unbearable.

Josh was dead and that was our reality. His girlfriend at the time was so torn at the funeral I wanted to wrap my arms around her. This was pain. This was what I had always protected myself from. Suicidal thoughts ran through my head. I couldn't eat, not even my favorite foods. Sleep was no longer a normal part of my life, and when it was it was during the day when the rest of the world was being productive. My drug use hit an all-time high and I could no longer function. Through Josh's death I learned that I cannot handle pain like "normal" people, whatever the "norm" is. This is why I couldn't love past my mind. I was too afraid of sincerely loving and losing. I honestly didn't think I'd live past this, but I had yet to discover my own strength.

As time went on, every day got easier. The memories of him never faded, and there wasn't a day that I didn't think of him. Still, I could finally eat and sleep through the sadness and no longer needed drugs and alcohol to get out of bed. I guess it's called "coping," and about six months after Josh's death I was coping pretty well. But as soon as I got into a good swing of life, yet another tragedy hit, too close to home.

Camille and I had been together for awhile, and she was there through these tragic events. Our relationship had its issues, as most do when young people try to be adults, but whether that girl had my back or not was never in question. During the time Camille and I were dating, we split up for awhile. That's the time I "dated" Shaun and she dated Briana.

I went back and forth about being with women exclusively, and Camille knew and understood. Nonetheless, while Shaun and I were seeing each other I got pregnant.

This came from out of nowhere. I didn't want this to happen. I was a rock star, and this whole pregnant thing didn't fit. Pregnant! Nothing I wanted to happen, but nothing I was trying to prevent from happening either. I was only twenty-two years old. I was not ready to be anybody's parent. Being a mom wasn't anywhere on my agenda. Still drinking, doing drugs, and smoking cigarettes, I wasn't ready to stop but I had to. It was hard for me to imagine there was a life forming inside of me that I now had to consider.

For a while, I was detached from the fetus and it worried me. But before long, I moved out from my godfather's house and went to make a home of my own for my kid. I stopped doing drugs and drinking almost instantly, but cigarettes were a little bit harder. I smoked for about three months of my pregnancy. By now Camille and I were back together so I didn't know if I wanted to tell Shaun or not. He and I weren't even in touch anymore. I didn't want the drama with Camille, but I never thought about what might be best for the baby. The other problem was I'd been messing with both Shaun and my ex-boyfriend, and I didn't know which one fathered the baby.

Early into the pregnancy, I started to have some complications. About the twenty-second week they found protein in my urine, which was too early to develop such an issue. They continued to watch me and warned me that if it grew worse, I'd be in the hospital on total bed rest. Young and full of energy, I didn't understand the full meaning or severity of what they were explaining to me. It became very real about week twenty-seven when I was admitted to the hospital for high levels of protein found in my urine. This could be fatal to my unborn fetus. Having just started to connect with my baby around twenty weeks when I realized it was a boy, I was scared. Visits from family members helped to ease my worry, but I was still afraid.

I was in the hospital for eight weeks, if I'm not mistaken. My family and friends were so supportive. Camille, bless her heart, drove all the way to our apartment, about fifteen miles away, every day and cooked me a feast because I hated the hospital food. If I was craving fish, she went to the sea to get it, fried it, and brought it back to me still hot. I couldn't say thank you enough. My Aunt Nell who worked in the hospital came to see me often and called to check on me at least twice a week. My sister came to braid my hair. My godfather taught me how to play spades finally. Tisha and KiKi came to visit with me and make me laugh. Malena came to visit, called, and checked the nurses because I didn't complain ever and the squeaky wheel gets the grease. My mom and dad came every other day and would not leave until Camille was back.

September 18, 2004, around 4 a.m., I was wide awake and couldn't sleep. I tossed and turned until I finally gave up and watched rerun marathons of *Fresh Prince of Bel Air* on TV. Suddenly a very odd pain stabbed me in the abdomen, and I noticed that my feet were the size of small watermelons. I informed the nurse that something had happened; they treated me for gas and that was that.

A few hours later I was in excruciating pain that went on and on. We finally realized I was in labor and the doctor came to check me. I was almost fully dilated and ready to push, but the baby boy, whom I had named Chance Amanté Seals, had flat-lined. Everything after that was a blur to me, as I had to be put to sleep for an emergency C-section. Just 34 weeks into the pregnancy, and weighing 5 lbs 11 oz, my baby never took a breath. He died in utero.

When I woke up in recovery, the first face I saw was my sister's. She was balling, but she still carried the strength of our mother. She kneeled down to me as she wiped her tears away and said, "Shalaunda, do you know what happened?" I said, "No, why are you crying?" She said, "My nephew didn't make it, he's dead. They tried to revive him for a long time, but he never took a breath." She rubbed my hands and said "I love you." Then in came Camille, my godfather, and my daddy, all looking so sad. Next came Shaun. I guess Camille called him once things turned urgent; she felt he should know. No matter who the daddy was, he was the father, period. Camille heard this from my own mouth and took it upon herself to call him. I respected her for that because I wanted to call him from the very beginning but worried about how she might feel. It didn't really register to me until the next day that my baby was dead.

I held my freezing cold baby—they had to refrigerate his body so he wouldn't begin to smell—and I wept. I was so hurt yet again I started to lose my mind. I became violent with the nurses and tried to harm myself. I snatched out the IVs and refused to take medicine that I needed. While in the hospital, I wouldn't eat, drink. All I did was cry. I made it through Josh dying and was just getting my life back from that. Now this! I was sure I was going to die and nothing anyone could do would save me. My mom read me Bible scriptures, told me Bible stories, sang to me...she did all she knew to do. It helped when she was around, but she couldn't be around 24/7. I often thought *if God knew this was going to happen, why let me get so attached and fall in love with Chance and the idea of being a mom?*

I wanted the pain to stop. WHY ME, WHY ME, WHY ME? When I finally came home I went to my godfather's house, not wanting to be reminded just yet of the home I was hoping to share with my firstborn son.

But even this was not the final tragedy to hit my life. It seemed as if death stalked everyone I loved—when would it end?

At certain points in my relationships with Tisha and KiKi, we didn't talk to each other as much but would hang out with other groups of friends instead. Tisha and KiKi both hung around girls that I didn't really know, and it seemed to happen mostly when we were not speaking. It was weird because most of the times we weren't upset with each other; we just did our own things sometimes. There were times when KiKi and Tisha were tight and I'd be doing my thing. Or KiKi and I were tight and Tisha would do her own thing. Nonetheless, we were best friends and nothing stopped that. We'd pick right back up where we left off as if nothing happened, and technically nothing did.

KiKi started hanging with a particular girl and guy that made me uncomfortable. The two weren't linked to each other I don't believe; she just started dating him and hanging with her around the same time. It's not that I didn't like them. I just felt that KiKi wasn't up to their speed, and she didn't have enough backbone to live the way they did, as I did. KiKi was passive, and you could convince her to do almost anything. Sound familiar? The girl she started hanging with was a dancer, but instead of working at a club, at the time she was dancing at house parties—never a good idea. Of course KiKi started dancing with her, and remember KiKi and I tried this; it was not her thing.

I told her I didn't agree with it and that she wasn't as street smart as the other girl, something you need to survive in the life she was about to unleash. People say that girl made her dance and whatnot, but you can't make another adult do anything. And if you know KiKi, you know she probably thought it was cute and asked to do it with her. KiKi would call and tell me what was going on, and I'd be so upset, though I didn't let her know I was. I did tell her to stop, but as I would do as well, she just pushed me away because KiKi was going to do what KiKi wanted to do.

Death Comes In Threes

We talked here and there during this era but not as often as we usually did. One day KiKi calls me telling me about this guy she was so in love with, as she was with many other guys in the past. KiKi wore her heart on her sleeve and often mistook many things for being in love. When she said his name, I instantly recognized it. I knew many people who had been in relationship with this guy, and I'd not heard very many good things about him.

As she went on and on about him, without knowledge of doing so, she was confirming everything I had heard. Afraid of being shut out of her life again, I just went with it. I listened to her go on and on about her life in the fast lane, and I knew deep in my heart she wasn't equipped for this. I lived in the fast lane for sure, but I knew not to put my heart into anything because the instant you start thinking with your heart you get caught up. KiKi didn't possess the toughness it took to live the life she was living, yet you couldn't tell her anything. And who was I to talk with all the negative things I was doing? When Josh died, my godfather had a talk with KiKi asking why we couldn't unwrap our minds from around this foolishness. He said that Josh's death would be in vain if we didn't learn from it and change our lives. Her reply to him was, "It's all we know."

Early March, a few weeks before KiKi's birthday, I got a call from Tisha, who was crying, crying, crying. KiKi had been shot in the back of the head but was still alive. Her boyfriend didn't make it, he died on the scene. Because it was a homicide and an attempted homicide, we weren't allowed to see her and her family shut everyone out which I can respect, so we knew the bare minimum. You can't imagine how hard it was to know that someone you loved so dearly was suffering in this way and you couldn't put your arms around them and hug them.

Violent crimes are never an easy pill to swallow, and being so far away made the situation even worse. I prayed, but not knowing much about the real power of prayer, it didn't help me. With every passing day I worried so much about KiKi, hoping she'd pull through. I couldn't focus on anything else. We finally heard from KiKi's sister that KiKi was in a rehab center and was doing better. We were all so thrilled to hear that she was improving. You can't imagine the relief we felt. I couldn't wait to see her, talk to her, hug her. I didn't care if she never talked the same again or if she never remembered who we were. A gunshot to the head can cause severe long-lasting trauma. I just wanted to lay my eyes on her and tell her how much I loved her.

Then, one day in early May, KiKi died from pneumonia. I remember her being sick and going to the ER around the time this happened, but I don't remember pneumonia. Maybe she developed pneumonia while lying in the hospital so long—I never asked—but my KiKi was gone. KiKi had a beautiful daughter that looks identical to her, and she would live the rest of her life without her mom. This was such a travesty my heart just couldn't take it. I kept my feelings inside, tired of crying and breaking down in front of the whole world. I didn't like the weakness that was on display so often now.

However, at home I was a wreck. Once again I couldn't eat or sleep, and getting out of bed was about impossible. I couldn't shower. I didn't want to speak to anyone. My life could have ended and I probably would have been okay with that, but my heavy heart I couldn't live with. KiKi's funeral was packed. I could barely look at her family without breaking down crying, especially her young daughter, bless her heart.

KiKi was a bright girl with a bright future ahead of her. Her life was taken away just like that...for what, we still don't know. I often wonder what she and Josh would be like if they were still alive. Everyone has changed so much. I wonder what type of people they would be. Over the years I've heard it was a drug deal gone wrong, or a setup by a family member, but I don't listen to any of it. Until her killer is brought to justice, only God knows.

KiKi's death tore me down—it was the last straw for me.

During the time while I was grieving the death of my son, Chance, my grandparents, Chris and Delores King, came to visit me. I was so happy to see them. They gave me a card and I read it when they left. To this day I have it tucked in my heart. This card made me weep so bad when I first read it, yet for some reason I read it every day. The name of the poem on this card was "The Oak Tree," and I may get some of the words wrong:

A mighty wind blew night and day,
and stole the Oak Tree's leaves away
Snapped its boughs, and pulled its bark
Until the oak was tired and stark

The Oak Tree said I know that you
Can break each branch of mine in two
Shake my limbs and make me sway
and carry every leaf away

But I have roots planted in this earth,
growing stronger since my birth
You'll never touch them for you see
They are the deepest part of me

Until today I wasn't sure
Of just how much I could endure
But now I've found with thanks to you

I'm stronger than I ever knew

Grandmother and PaPa, this card is what helped me heal during that difficult time in my life, and it meant so much more to me than I have ever told you. I read this card every day, four or five times a day, and cried my soul out every time I read it. You know the kind of crying where you can't speak or breathe for about twenty seconds? The kind of crying that when you're done you just want to go to sleep and you can hardly see because your eyes are so swollen? That is the kind of crying this card produced for me. Yet for some odd reason I could not stop reading it. Eventually I could read the card and tears would just fall. It got to a point where I didn't have to read it because I had the card memorized verbatim, so I would just think of it and start to tear up.

But do you know what began to happen with every tear? Healing... and I never knew it was happening. Don't get me wrong; it took years for me to understand the death of my son enough to fully recover from it, but the understanding that I needed to heal became possible through crying. My grandma used to say crying is like putting your soul in the washing machine. Though we may not like to cry, and most of us are too tough to do so, our healing starts with those tears we want to hold back.

To summarize these tragedies, Josh died first in 2003; Chance was next, stillborn in 2004; and KiKi was third in 2005. I could hardly mourn the loss of one loved one before another died. I was certain at this time in my life that I would lose my life or my mind, either one. Not that I am suicidal, I just didn't care. I had no will to live, and losing that made it hard for me to make good decisions.

I didn't understand Chance's death the most. Chance was a baby, pure and innocent. He had yet to make any decisions, especially bad ones that might cause an early death. Chance never got a chance to live, only inside of me. I spent months waiting to meet, hold, get to know, hear cry, see smile, smell, and love this baby boy, and I never even got to look in his eyes. The hardest line in the Oak Tree poem for me to read was "but now I've found with thanks to you, I am stronger than I ever knew."

Was I saying "thank you son for dying; you have given your mom strength"? It sounded twisted and it made me cry the hardest. I eventually learned why that had to happen, and I do thank my baby for making me realize my own strength. If I can say hi and goodbye to my firstborn child, I can do anything. If you have never been through it, you won't understand the pain it causes. You won't understand how big of a scar it can leave on a mother's heart.

These three deaths tore my heart to shreds. If you've ever lost a close loved one, you know that a year is still early. You just experienced all the first holidays without that person, and then somebody else dies the very next year and someone else the next. Most days I felt like a zombie walking among the living. The time between Chance's death and KiKi's death was the hardest to cope with, but something life-altering happened almost right after Chance's passing.

I came across a lump sum of money that could change my future, managed properly, and after the death of Chance, I was given this life changing amount of money, six figures. I had no idea what to do with all that money so of course I asked the most successful businessman I know: my godfather. Rod suggested I start a business, so most of the money he put away but a lot of it I blew. Camille and I went to Vegas and easily blew ten thousand dollars. Not only did I want to, I needed to. That vacation was just what the doctor ordered for me. Months of sleeping pills, therapy, and drugs, and this was all I needed. The problem was I could not live this life every day. I had to return home. And when I did, reality sank right back in.

My godfather did his best to keep me in good spirits and focused on anything except Josh and Chance. We often called around looking for a business we could invest in. Eventually we decided to open an ice cream shop. It was definitely more of what I was leaning toward because it sounded simple and I was nowhere ready for or wanting hard work.

The ice cream shop seemed like it was going to be the perfect business, and it was pretty easy to learn. I was the boss, a position I'd never want to be because it doesn't fit my personality. Bosses have to be firm, aggressive, and willing to take initiative. I am passive and worked best when following suit. Besides Camille and me, there was one employee and I liked her a lot. I found myself paying her more than she was owed because she started picking up all our slack. With Camille and me being the bosses, things spiraled fast. We started off just being late here and there to sometimes not coming in at all. I knew how businesses should be run from watching my godfather, but I didn't have enough drive or discipline to run a business myself.

We started slacking on ordering paper goods first, then being low on ice creams all the time. Soon our moneymaker, ice cream cakes, wasn't even a part of the business because we weren't keeping up on it. We expected this girl to pick up the slack, and she did as much as she could with what she had to work with. I knew it was over when we didn't have cups to serve the ice cream in. It was so embarrassing to have to face customers toward the end that we just stopped going.

My godfather got me out of the lease, and commercial leases can be a beast. Tired of making up lies for our childish behavior and dipping into our cash to keep it operating, we closed the ice cream shop after only one year of business.

What were we doing with all the money?

With everything going on with Josh and Chance, my drug use was at an all-time high, and so were my pockets from the extra money I had just come across. Me and whoever was with me got high when we wanted, as much as we wanted. Meanwhile, my life was at an all-time low. I hid myself away from family and friends because I was ashamed. I thought that after Chance I'd be done with cocaine forever, but the stress and pain made me want it more than ever.

One night we were chilling, getting high as we always did. The cocaine was good and so was the company, so instead of our usual Tylenol PM and lying there hoping to fall asleep, we got more coke. And more. And more. Until more turned into three days around-the-clock—sunup, sundown, sunup, sundown, sunup, sundown—and we were still snorting cocaine. I have no clue how much I spent, but I am certain our dealer was happy. No food at all, just water and cocaine. When we finally decided to stop, man oh man, I have never been so miserable. I felt weak, my nose was burning, and my heart was racing like nothing I'd never experienced before. I tried to lie down, but sheer panic made me sit right back up. Tried lying down again, but this time I felt like I was being smothered and could not breathe. Then I went into a full-on panic attack and could not breathe.

My friend, who was as high and crazy as I was, drove me to the hospital down the street. They had me waiting in the lobby for no longer than fifteen minutes, but it felt like hours. I thought I was going to die. These words will never allow you to feel how close I thought I was to death. I started to pray, "God, if You get me out of this, if You let me live, I will never do cocaine again. That is my word…I promise, I promise, I promise. God, I'm not ready to die, not like this." I began to think about my mom, my dad, my sisters and brothers, my friends, and I kept praying in my head.

Finally, I got back to a bed and the doctor asked me if I had been doing drugs. I replied, "YES YES YES, please don't let me die!" I think I told him it was my first time, I don't remember all the details, but I know I asked him to do whatever he had to do to keep me alive. He assured me I wasn't going to die. He gave me an IV with saline, turned the light off, and left me there. In less than one hour, I started to feel normal. Not only did my heart rate slow down, I felt 100 percent rejuvenated. I could have gone on another binge if I wanted to. Instead I drove home where everyone was still suffering. They had a long way to go in the coming-down process, and I told them all, "I am done with cocaine."

I'm sure none of them believed or even heard me, but to date those words have stood true. Cocaine would never be in my nose again. I only learn the hard way—no pain, no gain. And almost dying was painful, scary, and traumatizing enough.

My Message

My, my, how I couldn't wait to get to this part! Having to relive and expose things I have spent years trying to suppress hasn't been the easiest task, to say the least, but with the encouragement of a few friends and God on my side, I made it through. From the title of the book, you knew there had to be light at the end of the tunnel, and I am so elated to say, "Hello, my name is Shalaunda Nielsen, as I write this I am thirty years old, and I am SAVED, SANCTIFIED, AND FILLED WITH THE HOLY SPIRIT. I am sold out to the Lord and on fire for Him."

People who have met me in recent years don't believe half the things I tell them about my past. I take that as a compliment. I am nothing like I used to be or who the devil wanted me to be. God changed my life drastically, so let me tell you how it happened.

Over time I felt something telling me not to date women anymore. I had no idea what was happening inside me, but through my mom's helpful advice and evidence that I could not deny, I learned that God was pulling on my heart. I had been dating Melissa—that beautiful crazy girl I told you about earlier—but something was definitely happening to me. God knew me enough to know that for me to make it to Him, I had to be healed of past strongholds that would hinder me. Melissa and I split, and it was cut and dry. I never looked back.

Until I spoke with my mom, I thought it was all me deciding to change my life. I told my mom that Melissa and I had split and I didn't want another girlfriend. I informed her that I wanted to go to church and that I eventually wanted a husband. My mom was so happy she had to hang up on me and call me back. I didn't want my mom to be too excited and then I let her down and end up with another woman, so I stressed, "No guarantees, Mama, I just want to see."

We had a long talk that day, and I was surprised that talking about God didn't leave a bad taste in my mouth as it had every time in the past. Not too long after this talk, my mom went on a cruise for her anniversary. Meanwhile something life-changing was happening to me. I had been going to my mom's church every Sunday, and I really enjoyed it. It almost seemed like she had been telling the pastor my business because every sermon, every Sunday, ministered right to me. Was this a coincidence or was my mom telling this man to preach to me through his sermons?

I listened with an open heart and mind, but it seemed like the more I listened, the more I knew that this lifestyle was going to be too hard for me to live. And, only in my late twenties, I didn't want to lead a boring life like my mom and dad. I still liked to drink and go dancing at the club. I still thought women were sexy, though I didn't want to be with one. But I knew I'd always lust for them, and from what the pastor said about the lust of the eye, I knew I couldn't sit in church like that. So I just started talking to God. I didn't know how to pray, but in my conversations with Him I asked God what He wanted me to do. I don't know if I expected this blast of lightning or roar of thunder, and a deep powerful voice to say "I want you to yada yada yada...," but nothing happened. Nobody answered.

While at church one Sunday, the pastor asked those who wanted prayer to stand up, as he did every Sunday, but this Sunday I stood up. While praying, he said something about confessing Jesus Christ as our Lord and Savior and we would be saved. I repeated that with my mouth and with my heart, and I found out that day that Jesus was answering me the whole time. I couldn't wait for my mom and dad to come back so I could tell them I was saved and wanted to join a church somewhere.

My mom called when the ship touched land, and as I picked up the phone I said, "Mama, Mama, I have something to tell you." I was so excited and I knew my mom would be too.

As soon as my mom and dad got home, I rushed there to tell them the good news, and they were elated. My mom was jumping up and down, her eyes filled with tears, and my dad had the biggest smile on his face. I knew that finally this was something my parents would be proud of, and that alone made me glad. Now, being the honest person that I am, I told my mom that I didn't like her church because it was too old. There were hardly any people my age, and that didn't move me to want to join. She said, "There's nothing wrong with shopping for the right church that suits you. I love my church home, and I am not going anywhere, but to make sure you are somewhere they are preaching and teaching Jesus, I will go with you until you are settled in a church."

My mom knew the importance of being fed the Word of God properly. I decided to visit a few churches that my friends were members of, and I definitely felt more warmth at Ebenezer Missionary Baptist Church than any other. Another church I loved was full of young people, the music ministry was off the chain, and the pastor was the bomb, but the fellowship was too big. By the time I found somewhere to park and then a seat in the church, I had lost my religion ten times, and it took halfway through the service for me to find it again.

I found myself returning to the EMBC Sunday after Sunday, and though there weren't a ton of young people there, that pastor sure was preaching to me all the time, and that's what kept me going back. The week leading up to the Sunday I finally joined the church there, I had so much concern that I expressed to my mother, "How am I going to stop liking girls? Is God going to punish me for drinking and going out? Mama, I will still fight somebody if they make me mad. Will God be upset? I still love R&B and rap music, and I'm not gonna stop listening to it. Now what am I supposed to do about that?"

My mom gave the most innocent giggle as if my worries were not genuine, and she knew they were, but she also knew God—a God I had yet to discover. She said, "Baby, pray, and when you pray, remember you can't hide your heart and mind from God. He knows your every thought. Talk to Him like you are talking to me right now, and when you pray say, 'God, change my desires, take the desire out of my mouth for women.'" She assured me that if I wanted it gone, God would remove it. She said, "Get in relationship with Christ and He will handle the rest. Seek God, baby, don't you worry about anything else." How could she be so confident was my next question. Two people can do the very same thing and have completely different outcomes, so what if that worked for her but it didn't work for me?

I don't know if I believed that any of this was real or that people's minds were warped, but I heard my mom and my pastor say "trust God, try God" over and over. I said to myself, *Shay, if you can trust your godfather enough to get you to jump out of an airplane at 15,000 feet in the sky with a stranger attached to the front of you, or to bungee jump from 171 feet with nothing but a rope tied around your ankles going headfirst, you can at least try God and see what happens. Worst-case scenario, you end up right back where you started right?*

My biggest concern at this time was leading a boring life. Listening to Pastor and my mom, it was like, okay, well dark and light can't be on the same accord, but dark is where all the fun is. I'm just being honest. This is where I was at that point in my Christian walk. Giants, gods, devils, angels, demons, people rising from the dead and walking on water…I could go on. Greek mythology is what it sounded like to me. Might as well start talking about dinosaurs and evolution. Watching the church weep about these things was really hard to understand, but I decided to activate my faith. The size of a mustard seed was all I needed right? I decided to trust God, my mom, and my new pastor at Ebenezer Missionary Baptist Church. I didn't know what to do or where to start, but I was ready for change and I was trusting God.

Everyone in that church welcomed me with open arms, and I received them all with the same warmth. Instantly, my family grew that much more. Too shy and not being able to have a drink to relax before church, I didn't approach many people, but they all approached me with big smiles and even bigger hugs. Afraid that I would never measure up to the women at church every Sunday made me feel out of place. They were somewhere I was only trying to be, and I didn't fully believe that my ever being that "saved" was possible. When I joined church, my pastor assigned me to my mom and dad for discipleship training. I was happy with that because it was easier for me to open up to my parents. What God was about to do in, to, and for me was bigger than anything that has ever happened to me, and it totally struck me by surprise.

A Praying Mama

This is my testimony, but if you talk to my mom, you will see how it is hers as well. I lived in the world for almost ten years, and my mom prayed for what probably felt like twenty years. In retrospect, I can't imagine the worry I put her through, and nothing I did was a secret from my mom. I told her almost everything firsthand so she wouldn't have to wonder, as wondering is something I myself detested. But without knowing the heart of a mother, I had no idea the torture her mind and heart probably sustained. My mom never denied me when I was in the world. I could call and talk to her anytime about anything, within reason, and I was always welcomed in her home with open arms.

My mom never preached to me, or at me shall I say, because unless someone opens that door you are preaching at them not to them. Anyhow, she wasn't always jumping down my throat about what I was or wasn't doing, but she ended every conversation with "you know Mama is praying for you, and I love you." My mom would also leave me voicemails when I didn't answer the phone singing, "You are my sunshine, my only sunshine, you make me happy, when skies are gray, you'll never know dear, how much I love you, please don't take my sunshine away." I could hardly listen to the voicemail without weeping.

Just as God knows us, our mothers do as well. I wasn't the kind of child and still am not the kind of adult that responds to yelling and anger. I have a heart; all you have to do is speak to it.

I believe with my whole heart that when I was in the world, my mom's prayers are what covered me, and they are also what brought me back home. Ephesians 6:4 (KJV) says, "And, ye fathers, provoke not your children to wrath: but bring them up in the nurture and admonition of the Lord." My mom proclaims that I was such an obedient submissive child that she knew when I submitted fully to the will of God, I'd have no problem obeying Him. I don't know how she knew that, but my obedience to God is first in my life and non-negotiable. I may plead my case and stick my bottom lip out, but ultimately what God says goes. Then I tuck that bottom lip in and remember that He wants only what's best for me. How can I be mad at that? So I smile and say, "Thank You, Lord, for Your correction."

I was raised in a Holy Ghost-filled, Jesus-loving, preaching-and-teaching home and family. If we didn't learn anything else at home, we learned to fear God. Believe it or not, when I was in the world I feared God enough not to play with Him, so I dared not step my foot in a church. I went to church for funerals, and one time my dad convinced me to go on Mother's Day, and I mean one time.

What protected me from harm all those nights and in all those fights? Drinking, drugging, and driving, not remembering how I got here or there, and I've never been in a wreck and never had a DUI. Promiscuous behavior for years, and I've never had an STD. Overcoming drug habits that have people on the streets prostituting themselves and losing everything. I walked away from cocaine and never looked back. People say I didn't have a habit, I just used to experiment. I'm sorry God made quitting look too easy so some people won't believe it was a habit. Not only did I have a habit, I should have been in and out of rehab for the amount of drugs I used, BUT MERCY SAID NO.

God kept me because my mom was faithful to Him, and she

NEVER stopped praying for me. God heard her cries. The Bible says in James 5:16b (KJV), "The effectual fervent prayer of a righteous man availeth much." Surely it wasn't my own prayers that kept me, but my mom's faithfulness and diligence. I only prayed when I felt like my life was in danger and I was scared. I didn't practice praying, but I always said grace before eating a meal. My mom says all the time, "I live my life sold out to the Lord. I need too much from Him to be playing. I need my children covered and saved, and it's too many of y'all for me to half-step."

My mom tells me frequently how proud of me she is, and I always think to myself, *What did I do?* Parents want to be proud of their children; it speaks a lot of the parent when the child succeeds or fails. My mom says parents are proud to say "that's my kid" when they graduate college, get married, and walk in the image of God. But when things don't look so good, they don't know where they got that behavior from. Your failures are mine and so are your successes, says my mom.

Though people always told her they saw me and I looked good, or I had a new car, or maybe I gave them some money, my life was not an honorable one. My mom was probably thinking *wipe that money off if you got it from my daughter*, though she smiled and kept the conversation flowing. People would say, "Man, we heard about Shalaunda dating women and stripping. Think she might be doing drugs too. What are you going to do?" I can only imagine my mom's face when she said, "What do you mean what am I going to do? I am going to love her and keep praying for her. I don't have any kids to give away." Then she'd ask them, "What are you going to do about that son/daughter of yours that keeps making kids and they're not married? Or that son who's selling drugs or the daughter who's doing them?" My mom is not one to mess with, especially about her kids, and if you know her, you know she can hold her on.

I learned so many things from my mom and still learn from her every day, especially now that I too am sold out to the Lord and we converse about nothing but the goodness of Jesus. I am so thankful to my mother for being an example of what a God-fearing woman should look like and always loving me right where I was. If I could say anything to my mom, it's that I owe you my life, literally. Not because you raised me as a kid—okay, that too—but because you never gave up on me when the rest of the world did. Every time I spoke to you and called you in the middle of the night strung out, you gave me something that a person like me didn't feel worthy of: hope.

Mama, forgive me for the lies I told to fit in because everyone else was talking about what rough lives they had and I didn't want to be left out. Thank you for understanding me and always taking up for me, no matter how much it may have embarrassed you at times. You are the reason I live, for more reasons than one. Thank you for continuing to pray when it looked like I was totally lost and never to return. Only a mother... You could have been praying for a Benz or to be rich, but what you were praying for was obvious: me. Your passion, your patience, your faithfulness I never deserved, but you gave it so freely. For being the wisest person I know and always thinking before you speak, apologizing if you're wrong, and calling back ten times in a row when you knew you were right and I may not have wanted to hear it, but needed to—nobody can tell you like your mother.

I love you, Berta D. Not only do I look like you, I desire to be just like you. One day we will have to put you in the ground, and it will be the hardest goodbye I ever have to say, so I choose to give you your flowers now while you are here. Anything I can do for you, I find an honor and a privilege. I truly appreciate and am grateful for you. Thank you for everything, and thank you most of all for consistently praying.

Conviction, Not Comfort

I just told you how when I started going to Ebenezer Missionary Baptist Church, it seemed like my pastor was always preaching directly to me and no one else. For a while I believed my mom really was telling him certain things, but then I learned a little more about God and how He works. I knew for sure then I was in the right church home. Everything that was a worry in my mind, or things that I somehow justified (you know how we do), my pastor cleared it up on Sunday morning. Slowly but surely I got convicted by the Holy Spirit about everything in my life that needed to change.

The word *convicted* was very popular in the early parts of my new relationship with Christ. My friend and I stood corrected or convicted about something new every Sunday. One of my friends I had grew close to at the time was a member of Canaan Worship Center her Pastor was hitting home for her as well. It was awesome. Unlike some people who turn their heads like, *uh-oh, was he talking about me...no one knows I do that*, we liked to know what was wrong and what was right. That way we could choose our battles. We'd call each other at least weekly saying "do you think I do this or that?" I loved that about our conversations, especially at that time in our lives when we needed to learn and grow as believers.

How am I to know what I am supposed to be praying for and trying to change if someone doesn't correct me? Then after that correction comes conviction, and I don't know about you, but I'd rather stop at correction from a sermon by my pastor than conviction from God. God is our Father, so naturally He treats us like our parents. If we don't know, He makes sure we find out (living in His will of course). Once we know and choose to do the opposite, here comes the belt. Sometimes I wish God could just whoop me with a belt because that would seem easier than the heaviness my heart feels when He has to check me.

God knows exactly how to deal with every one of us, and He definitely knows how to get to Ms. Shay's heart. Guilt for me is the ultimate punishment, and wronging God, who is incapable of hurting me (temper tantrums with God when I don't get my way don't count), is one of the hardest feelings for me to overcome. When God first started convicting me, I'd beat myself up and feel so unworthy (which I am), but the true feeling of unworthiness will weigh you down. I didn't know how to forgive myself and my shame knew no end. But what a mighty God we serve, because He allowed me to feel His forgiveness so I could pick myself back up and try my very best not to make that same mistake (true repentance).

I thank God for my pastor and thank my pastor for allowing God to use him to preach and teach directly to me. Had my Pastor not been correcting me, and worried more about making me comfortable or getting my tithes faithfully (forget my soul and teaching me how to get to heaven), it's very possible that I'd still be lost. Thank you Pastor Frazier; for being a man of integrity and good morals. You and Mama Shirley, my beautiful first lady who is ninety-eight pounds of pure sugar, have led by example, and been such an inspiration to my family and me.

I was in the world for most of my adult life thus far, so I associate with lots of people who have yet to be delivered. God pulls on us all at different times; and I pray everyone grabs the rope when He starts pulling.

You name the sin, I have an acquaintance for it; I am not judging, I'm speaking matter-of-factly. Some of these acquaintances are in church on a regular basis. I don't ask people and I don't preach at people, but if you listen to someone long enough you will find out what you need to know, what you didn't want to know, and what you need to pray for.

"We go to church where we are comfortable," they say to me. "My pastor doesn't preach about *all that*. Yes, I am in my mess, but I am on the usher board, I sing in the choir, and I'm on the praise and worship team. My pastor knows what I do and he doesn't judge me." My response is always a polite one as I am not rude, condescending, or judgmental, but I am in no hurry to visit that fellowship.

I can't stress the importance of people in leadership and ministry being in a right relationship with Christ themselves and *their* leaders holding them accountable. If a young man comes to our church and he's living with a young lady, not married to her and knocking her up every year, and the minister or even the drummer he knows personally is doing the exact same thing, what's going to encourage that young man to change? Being active in ministry says, to me anyway, "look at me, follow my example, this is what a man or woman of God should look like, I set the standard." We may never see that young man again, and was he not just led astray? Did someone not just tell him without telling him that what he is doing is perfectly okay?

I can go on and on with scenarios, but I think we get the gist of it. If that same young man walked into our church and saw the same minister or drummer he knows well enough to know they share similar stories, but he sees that guy in the pews, do you know what that might say to the young man, in my opinion? It would say, "I'm not the only one who's trying to get it right...old boy is thinking just like me." One of those scenarios is productive, the other counterproductive, and as Christians the last thing we want people to be is misguided.

When people judge the church as a whole and say "I know people who go to church every week faithfully and still do this or that," I would hope they are talking about people who sit in the pews; but sadly if that were the case, the church wouldn't leave such a bad taste in people's mouths.

I consider my whole life a ministry, and every time I see someone I used to know and they say "hey, Shay, there's something different about you," I'm not only walking in my ministry, I'm succeeding in my ministry, and if God never calls me to do anything else, I am perfectly happy being a light. I'm fine with people watching my walk. I will make sure I keep cute shoes on for you. Nonetheless, we have to do better as mature believers at not leading people astray, but bringing them into relationship with Christ.

I am observant; I watch a lot and speak very little, and I have noticed problems with the church that many seasoned believers probably already know about, but being a baby in my salvation, I am troubled by this. I am no one to give advice to anyone in leadership, and please forgive me if I sound authoritative, but we've got to do better. One of my favorite gospel artists, Kirk Franklin, says in a song titled "Wake Up" that whoever has the microphone, remember the blood is on your hands. That statement alone gives me shivers. It's not a position I'd want to be in; one wrong word and someone's soul could be lost forever. God forbid, but is that not the worst-case scenario?

Quit worrying about making people comfortable for whatever reason and focus on their eternal resting place. You've got to make sure you are preaching and teaching the right things, AT ALL COST. Ephesians 4:11-15 speaks for itself, and if the King James is difficult for you to understand, search for a different rendering, but stay in the word of the living God. If I were a member of a fellowship and I was yearning to get right with Christ and some of the above things were happening, I'd never come back. People who are still in their mess cannot minister to me and shouldn't be ministering to anyone else. Again, I come in peace and mean everything I say with all due respect.

To my peers who have decided to live for Christ, remember that our youth look to us as examples more than they do older believers. Most youth think that older people are just bored, and "I will get my life right when I am old too; what else will there be to do?" It is so important for us to lead them properly and make sure we are not just an example, but a good example of young people on fire and living totally for the Lord. It's awesome to want God to use us and be anxious to do His work, but get fed first before you think you are in a position to feed. Learn all you can, and can all you know.

In my opinion it's a bad idea to get saved one day and start preaching and teaching the next. There's so much to learn that we need to dedicate our time as baby believers, learning from those in leadership, concentrating on our private devotions, and learning to hear God and how He speaks to us. We all want to get saved and just take over the church or start our own church, but there is a divine order to this. People have been doing this long before us, and it is honorable and expected for us to follow their lead.

We all want to whine about "old people" doing everything in church, but old people pay tithes. Old people are reliable and understand that it's our job to take care of our pastors. Old people aren't in the club shaking a tail-feather one day and praising Jesus the next. God will call us to do what He wants us to do, be patient. Until then, get your heart, your life, and your household in line with the Word of the true and living God.

Married To God and Him

My mom teaches a class to women titled "Married to God and Him," and I've discussed with her some of the things she reviews in this class. I am begging her to teach another one. Being delivered from homosexuality meant that my search for a husband had to begin. Or shall I say I needed to get ready as my husband was searching for me. The Bible says in Proverbs 18:22 (KJV), "Whoso findeth a wife findeth a good thing, and obtaineth favour of the Lord." I may take that scripture too literally, but when He said *find*, to me it meant I could just live my life and the right man would spot me and pick me out of a crowd.

But how was I supposed to know who this man was? Should I say yes to anyone who said "God told me you're my wife"? Discernment, what's that? This was going to be new territory for me considering the fact that I hadn't been in a serious relationship with a man since Trouble when I was nineteen years old; over eight years ago. I didn't even know what kind of man I liked physically, or what type of personality would blend well with mine.

Listening to my mom, she just sounded as if she was on repeat from all the stuff she told me when she found out I was interested in boys at age fourteen. But wait, there was one crucial fact: I didn't listen to her then and look where I ended up. My rebellion did not work out in my favor to say the least. I remember the day this thought first entered my mind. I picked up the phone and called my mom.

I listened to her that day almost to the point of taking notes. The first words I remember were, "Act like a *lady*, Shalaunda, and you will get a *man*, but don't portray something that you can't live up to. If you're a lady, be one all the time, not just until you get the ring." *Yes, ma'am* was what I was thinking. My mom gives it to you straight, my favorite way. Then she went on to say, "If you want a husband and not a ten-year boyfriend, keep your legs closed. If you have problems, take it to the Lord in prayer, but be nothing short of a lady and you will become a wife. After marriage, the Bible says in Hebrews 13:4, 'Marriage is honourable in all, and the bed undefiled: but whoremongers and adulterers God will judge.'" Finally, she told me to learn how to cook and said I could come over to her house and watch her cook any day, as I should have been doing when she was trying to teach me as a little girl.

Man, I cried standing in that hot kitchen sweating as she cooked. I complained until she put me out, and guess what? I went to clean up as happy as could be. She said, "You are already a very clean person, you clean up as good as I do, but you need to be able to prepare a meal for your family, especially your husband." I just did not want to hear that, and I knew she was going to say it, but I listened and I learned how to do enough to get by. We talked about a few more things, but that's the important stuff.

Suddenly I seemed to be the star actress in the movie *50 First Dates*, and not because I couldn't remember dating, but because it seemed like I was racing to fifty. Almost half the guys who asked I went on a date with, and it was a few. On my mom's advice, I made the guys agree to meet at a particular restaurant/bar, with me arriving fifteen or twenty minutes before the time I told them to meet there. The staff was pretty good about watching out for me.

Since I got off work at 10 p.m., it didn't look bad to meet for drinks so late, but I'd stay for no longer than an hour, if it were going well, and only one cocktail. My mom said, "It's not fair to date so many people at once because you might dismiss someone for doing something you don't like just because you have so many options. What if the one you dismiss because he didn't open a door was the right one, but Casanova has learned how to seduce a woman's panties off? And 'Jake' is genuine but has never been with a lady with those standards? You willing to fire Mr. Right because of something he can be taught and end up with Casanova, who plays this game by memory now?"

Good point, Mom. I knew then I had to narrow it down.

Having matured a little bit, though I still didn't know my "type," I knew what I didn't want—a hood boy—but I liked a man with a certain swagger about himself. I liked a man with power who was in control of himself if nothing else. I liked a man whose strength could compare to mine. My godfather demanded I find a man who could take care of me, and that doesn't mean me sitting on my butt and saying "give me," but not me taking care of other people and him taking care of me. But above all else, he had to be honest.

One of my co-workers hooked me up with this guy he had tattooed a few times and thought was a great catch. I met him, okay saw him, but he was a prude and I had no second thought of him. Very attractive young man, but very dry and seemed uptight. Of course, it would be so sweet if I said that once I got to know him, he was down-to-earth and romantic. Don't hold your breath; when a man is interested in a woman, you usually can tell. Between you and me, I still don't believe he was interested. I think he just entertained the thought after my co-worker put it in his mind. That's how cold his demeanor was or how hard he was to read, and I don't believe anyone is that unreadable.

I'd eat McDonald's and he'd say "gross" in a rude, condescending way. Oh God, when I first lit a cigarette, he looked like I had the plague and was contagious. I'd dated guys who don't like cigarettes before. They try their best to keep a straight face as they let you know how *not sexy* that cigarette is. I knew for sure this man didn't like me because he did absolutely nothing to impress me. Not that I wanted him to be fake, but I like to see the softer, flirty, lighthearted side of a person before all else. Though it seemed rude and he was very hard to connect with, I liked it. I'm all about honesty and the choice to keep dating him proved that. He was not only honest in what he said but in who he was; his actions were genuine—rude but genuine.

Another guy I was dating had enough swag for everyone reading this book to buy some, but he started off doing the right things and ended up being stuck on himself, so that dead-ended. I was looking for something serious and wasn't about to waste any more of my time with someone who wasn't promising. Like my mom always says, we date to mate, not just to have experiences.

The handsome, Express model-looking, distant, and cold man's name was Colter. His authentic "I am who I am, take it or leave it" personality was magnetic to me. Every one of my friends has asked me what I see in him. Colter does not have a personality that will win everyone over, but in reality that was ideal for me. There are tons of people I associate with, but few I call friends. I have a passion for people, and I am kind to all. It takes a lot to get me to dislike you. But only two of my friends had ever been to my home, and they were the only two who even knew where I lived. If I reciprocate the word *friend*, I know the depth behind it, and it's not an idle word for me.

I reserved the real me for very few, making Colter's and my hermit hearts the ideal match. He didn't talk much even when we were alone. I quickly discovered that when he talks he offends, and that's probably why he doesn't talk much. Most of us spend years trying to say things in ways that won't hurt someone else's feelings, or won't come off as rude and condescending. I did anyway, but not him.

Colter isn't from Kansas City, and most of his time spent here was spent alone. He had a few girlfriends, a few friends from college, but he never grew close to anyone, giving him the character of a hermit. He never took me to meet any of his friends, and the only people he ever talked about were his family. By the time we met in 2009, a few years out of college for him, he lived life totally alone. It was so odd to me that someone could live this way, especially after always having a huge entourage myself. How could you just hang around no one but yourself?

Colter and I dated a few months, and I started liking him unaware of it even happening. Without a ton of personality, sense of humor, and charm (things women usually go crazy over) there was nothing for me to write about in my diary. Gradually we started to hang out even more, and I really liked him by now. Before we knew it, we had keys to each other's places and he was washing my car and I was doing his laundry. We shared the same hopes and dreams for the future, and we got along well.

Five months into dating, we realized that we wanted to be in each other's lives every day. We were abstaining from sex as well, and that was becoming difficult with all the time we spent together. Combined, we paid over two thousand dollars in rent/mortgage monthly. What were we supposed to do now? Colter was definitely a God-fearing man and a member of a local church here in Kansas City. I was fresh into my walk with Christ and scared of messing up, so living together without being married was out of the question. But from the world's standards (which were still mine as well…it was all I knew; I was learning the rest) you have to be dating about two years before you even consider marriage.

My Pastor quoted a scripture in one of his sermons Sunday Morning that really caught my attention. The scripture was 1 Corinthians 7:9, "but if they can not contain, let them marry: for it is better to marry than to burn." When my pastor said that, I thought he was talking about burning in hell, but while casually conversing with my mom I brought up the topic and she said, "Oh, baby, it means to burn with lust, not burning in hell." My eyes opened a little bit wider because this was a handsome man we're talking about here.

I wanted it broken down all the way. What's lust? I mean, he's cute! I had to quit playing crazy trying to justify reasons because surely this Bible wasn't telling me to marry someone I hardly knew just because I lusted over him. Later that same night, Colter and I had a talk about marriage and what God expects. I thought for sure we were going to be done because I had to put my foot down and say no sex until marriage. Colter was a bit combative, but I told him what my mom had been telling me every time I asked her something: pray about it.

God must have put a bug in his ear because one month later, July 5, 2009, Colter's parents were in town for the Fourth of July, and we wanted our parents to meet. I thought it was just a casual meeting, but the next thing I knew Colter was getting down on one knee and his nephew Dylan was handing him a ring box. Tears filled the room as everyone overflowed with joy. I thought no one knew except Colter and Dylan, but I later found out that Colter asked my parents for my hand in marriage, and they did a good job at not telling me. Even I am impressed. I should have known by the huge smiles they wore whenever I saw them during the weeks leading up to the engagement. I have never felt more respected, more cherished, or more adored than Colter made me feel that day.

Before ever allowing him in my bedroom, I had a ring, and we're not talking about a little pawn shop ring here—those who know jewelry know. I won't tell you the carat weight (I don't want to get beat up on the way to my car) but I've never been more impressed, felt more special, and recognized my actual worth until that moment.

Colter and I decided to get married at the end of August, which was just a little over a month away, and have a big ceremony later. He knew I was the one when he took his time and spent his money on my ring. And I knew he was the one when I said yes. And the truth was we were paying too much money living in separate places, and our money was soon to become one. Besides, he was getting cuter every time I saw him. We wanted to please God, but we were also melting—we were burning so hot if you get my drift.

On August 30, 2009, I became Mrs. Colter P. Nielsen, all glory be to God. I say glory to God because during those six weeks I changed my mind ten times. Colter was a man of a certain stature, and the same things I loved about him were the same things that made me want to call it off. Colter went to college and was pretty much the ideal kid, not making very many mistakes in his life. He was disciplined, he was motivated, he was everything I wasn't JUST YET and definitely wasn't in past years. He had a substantial savings, good credit, and he owned his home, so he definitely wanted to know where I stood on paper within forty-eight hours of our engagement.

Who pushed the panic button, because that's exactly what I did. I was blowing my brains out using drugs every day...does he think I was worried about credit or savings when I was making all these terrible mistakes? Yes, I made good money, but I didn't save it, I gave it away and did whatever I wanted to do with it. Oh yeah, put it in my nose. I did not want this man to know what a failure I was, and feelings of inadequacy overwhelmed me. I didn't deserve this quality of a man and I knew that. I thought, *Somewhere in this world there's a girl as harmless as he is who deserves a man of this stature.*

I shared my feelings with my mom, and she said, "Shalaunda, the old you didn't deserve this man. The old you wasn't even thinking about men. Do you love him and are you willing to give him all you got? Are you prepared to listen to him, because he can teach you a lot. As long as you are on his team and let him be the captain (as long as he's leading the ship to Christ) and listen to and trust his correction and advice, you do deserve him and you guys will grow and learn together."

My mom's talk did help and made me feel a little better, but I still would ask God, "Are You sure this is the man for me? He's too good for me, and I don't want to bring him down." I'd tell God how I didn't want to be his baggage. I was all too familiar with the feeling from everyone allowing me to put all their weight on my shoulders. I was learning at this time that God knows the heart and we can't hide it from Him. Since that was true, I prayed to God and knew I could release insecurities to Him that I'd never tell anyone else.

One day Colter asked me to pull a copy of my credit report and give it to him. My heart began to beat fast, my palms got sweaty, but I smiled and said, "Okay, you know it's not good." Truthfully, I had no idea what was on there. I had never viewed my credit report, never had a reason to, never cared to be perfectly honest. I was a cash-and-carry type of girl, got it from my godfather. I worried and worried and worried some more. Then I remembered my Uncle Kevin saying when I was younger, "If you're going to worry, don't pray; and if you're going to pray, don't worry."

I tried to stop worrying and start praying, but the worry consumed me. I wasn't worried about him judging me; Colter was a God-fearing man, so if he were to judge, God would convict him right? Remember I was learning and I knew what conviction felt like to me, so surely it felt the same for everyone. My worry was that he already loved me and we were engaged, but had he seen my credit report sooner, maybe he would have made a different choice.

IT IS IMPORTANT TO ME THAT PEOPLE ARE ABLE TO MAKE UP THEIR OWN MINDS. Life is about choices. We've got to allow people to decide for themselves what they will and won't put up with. I did tell him from the very beginning that I had bad credit, but maybe I didn't stress just how bad. I didn't really know the extent of it. So I was definitely afraid of seeing my report for myself, and I couldn't even imagine what his first thought was going to be. Probably *give me my ring back, I made a mistake.* And it was nothing he said or did that made me assume such, just insecurities.

What a mighty, faithful, matchless God we serve. I pulled that report and there were seven to nine hospital bills in collections, and the amount of the debt was less than $2500 total! I wanted to do two things: put on my dancing shoes to praise God openly and write somebody a check. THANK YOU, JESUS! The testimony gets even bigger, but let me continue to make this point first. The same reason I was worried was the same reason I was happy: my credit wouldn't be a burden to my future husband! I could pay that off before he and I ever needed my credit for anything. That was my biggest concern, and with that behind me I could let my fears go and enjoy loving and being loved. We were married, and I thought I would get the "happily ever after" fairytale. Boy was I in for a surprise.

Who Stole My Fairytale?

*I*n just one short week, I thought I moved in with a demon. If I knew then what I know now, it would have saved a lot of drama, but we have to go through to learn the lesson (especially me), and I learned. There's a part to this that I will leave out because it might need a book by itself. Maybe the ladies and I can get together and talk about that on a more personal level, if that part of the testimony may help someone else. Nonetheless, there's a lot to be said about us women and our unrealistic expectations of men.

Colter and I had only been dating six months before we were husband and wife, so there was a lot we didn't know about each other. The first night I slept at his house, it was *our* house and he carried me over the threshold. It was an awesome feeling; I'm glad I listened to Mommy. Everything was so much more special because we did it the right way. But after only six months of dating, there was still so much to learn. My baby, bless his heart, went on about his normal life as if I didn't exist. We didn't discuss dinner ideas together—he just ate and I was left to fend for myself in what was a strange environment to me.

Colter watches sports obsessively, and I'd get off work and sit next to him waiting for him to ask about my day, rub my feet...I mean I felt like Casper, except that on the inside I felt everything but friendly. This went on for over two months, and I was heated with rage from feeling neglected, not needed, and, worst of all, unwanted. Most of the time he would hardly look up and talk to me, so I started to pursue outside interests myself. I became a Facebook junkie, and all I did when we were home together was talk on the phone or text. Colter never said a word, like asking who I was talking to, why I was talking to them, and what we were talking about. I realized that he didn't care because he wanted his life to stay the same as if I never entered it. He never told me that, but that's what his actions said.

I felt like a kid who had been moved from their happy home to a home with a stepparent that hated them. Colter never complimented me when I'd get all dolled up, and I don't care what any woman says, it's all done for her man if she has one. I couldn't get a feel for what he liked because he never said anything. Ladies, you know what I'm talking about. When our man says, "Oh, baby, you really look nice in that," we start to buy more things in that style, that color because it's all for them. Work clothes, church clothes, after 5 p.m. clothes, bedtime clothes, no clothes… he never said a word about anything.

On top of that, we had another problem. Colter is a frugal man, and I respected that—his discipline is why he is so accomplished, and my mom and godfather opened my eyes to that—but it was the opposite of me. I started to feel like nothing more than a number. I'm not bashing my husband; keep reading and learn what God can do. He was upset with me about every dollar I spent. No, I am not frugal like he is by any means, but these are all things I did to and for myself before him. Why would I get married to be anything less than what I've been in the past? But I didn't put up an argument as I am a passive person.

Instead I was growing to hate him, as I have everyone else in my past from letting things fester. Then one day I realized something as I was complaining to my mom about the things that were upsetting me. I love this man! I didn't marry him to give him away. There was no way this was going to work if I didn't communicate with him. Our pastor went over this with us in marriage counseling, and I knew I had to talk to Colter about the issues and give him the opportunity to fix them. It's unfair to sit around being hurt and someone not know it, and by the time they realize it you're numb from the pain of hurting and ready to walk out the door. Give someone the chance to say "I don't care what or how you feel," but first you have to tell them how you feel.

One of my biggest flaws in relationships is communication. I know it, I've known it since Josh, but no matter how much I know it's a problem, I can't change it. The more things hurt my feelings, the more silent I'd become; the more things built up, the more I couldn't wait to leave. When I express my feelings, the thoughts seem to disappear and I get over them quickly. I knew this, but no matter how much I tried everything was better left unsaid.

At one point Colter and I had a huge argument, and I called my godfather and told him what was going on. His first response was, "Have you told Colter this?" Well, of course I hadn't. I knew what was coming next. "Shalaunda, you're not a little girl. It's time to put on your big girl shoes and learn that you have to communicate or no relationship is ever going to work, PERIOD," he said, yelling at me because he was frustrated that I was crying and upset. Rod went on to say that Colter was a great guy and he (my godfather) approved of him, and that should speak volumes to me, as it did. My godfather is a man, and he will call a boy a boy any day of the week. He let me know the same thing my mom did: "Colter isn't a psychic; you have to tell him what you like, need, and want, and then when he doesn't do those things, you can feel like this. You are hurting yourself by keeping things to yourself when you're not in a relationship with yourself."

I tried telling Colter how I felt a few times, and at first it was the ultimate fix. Then he started to feel like all I did was complain, and things just turned into an all-out shouting match. I don't yell, I fight. I found myself starting to hit him, and two things happened: I realized this was how my previous relationships turned violent and why I wanted out of them so badly. Though I could bring the drama, I didn't want the drama. And in the same week that I told my mom and godfather that I hit Colter, they both said the exact same thing (like they always do): "Shalaunda, you cannot hit that man. That is a *man* and you don't hit like a girl. If you get him mad enough that he decides he wants to fight you back, you cannot overpower him no matter how tough you think you are. This is not a door you want to open in your marriage."

It made sense, a lot of sense, but I still learn things the very hard way, not just hard. When Colter and I went out one night to a local nightclub, things got messy and fast. I don't remember all the details, but we were fighting in public and the police got involved. I was mad that people saw that side of us. Though we were fighting what seemed like a lot, this part of our marriage didn't last but a few months. We even got in a huge fight on the night of our wedding ceremony, and his parents were there—that was embarrassing.

All these incidents were alcohol-induced, or rather they resulted from me holding things in and the alcohol bringing them out. Now there was a new problem: me telling Colter how I felt and him not taking it well but getting defensive. Colter always thought it was about me wanting to be right, but if you know me you know better than that. He had yet to know me on this level. The reason I like truth and I give truth is because that is how we grow; it's what makes us better. What are we in each other's lives for if we can't make each other better? And how do you do that if you take someone's voice from them?

My mom brought up a good point one day, and I thought *why didn't I think of that?* She said, "Why don't you try to talk to his mom. Colter is a great guy, but no woman has ever demanded the best out of him. He's been in Kansas City alone for so long, and that says a lot about his character right there. He can live his life alone and that's not a bad thing; he just needs to learn a different way. He needs to learn to share his world in a way that he hasn't had to before. Talk to his mom and open your heart to her. She will hear and listen to you. The same way your godfather and I take up for Colter and come down on you, I'm sure his mom will do this as well." That's when I learned my husband's most valuable asset, his true net worth: his mom.

I texted my mother-in-law and told her I needed to talk to her, and she called me back instantly. I gave her a brief description through the text of what I wanted to talk about, and I didn't know how to feel about the fast response. She sounded so warm it was refreshing. You never know how a mother is going to react to your saying her child is anything less than perfect. I learned my mother-in-law's genuine heart through our marriage's rough times.

I informed her of everything going on with her son, and I assured her that I loved him and wanted it to work out. But I knew it wouldn't work like this, no matter how badly he or I wanted it to. She assured me that she would talk to him, and she even apologized for the way I was feeling.

I don't know what my mother-in-law said to my husband, her youngest son, but he came home from work that day with a completely different attitude. WOW! Who was this man, and what had he done with my husband? He apologized for his behavior and assured me that he'd be willing to listen from then on. For the longest time we didn't even raise our voices at one another for anything. Colter was so attentive to my needs I was floored by his response. More than floored, I was grateful.

I never asked him or her what she said, but it worked. A grown man that will listen to his mother to this extent has got to be a good man—he just needs some tightening up around the edges. And a mother-in-law who will listen to the cry of her daughter-in-law and do her best to resolve the issue and keep the peace and not create more drama is a mom to me by action, not just on paper.

From then on I knew I could call her and talk to her about any problems I was having with Colter. To date, I haven't taken advantage of that. I am so grateful for my Nielsen/Phillips side of the family. Combining families can be trying, but because of their understanding and down-to-earth personalities, my family has grown to more than my heart and arms can hold. I have never felt anything less than loved while in their hometown, and my gratefulness is never ending. I was so afraid I wouldn't measure up to the kind of girl they wanted for their son. I felt as if my past were written on my forehead and everyone could read it. Even though I knew I had changed, my shame weighed heavily on me. I told my mother-in-law just about everything I'd ever done in the past, and she has never judged me. She has always gone out of her way to make sure I was comfortable.

Colter used to always say "you act like my mom," which I've heard is a good thing and the first sign I was getting the ring. If the saying is true that every man grows up to marry his mother, I'm honored. Her shoes are too big for me to ever truly fill, but if I naturally act like her, then I have a head-start right? To date, we are like best friends. We understand each other, and our relationship is not predicated on Colter; she is my mom because I love her and she loves me

As I write this, Colter and I have been married almost three years, and God has done nothing but bless us. He is my best friend, and no one understands me like he does. We're not the type of people that have to be in someone's face 24/7. He respects the things that make me Shay, and I respect the things that make him Colter. We are both independent and headstrong, and I know he is my husband and I am his wife. Anyone else would probably declare that he or I didn't need them or have time for them and leave.

I also found out that Colter actually complimented me from the very beginning—he is just a man of very few words. Nonetheless, he now vocalizes his compliments and I relish them all. I buy whatever I want/need, within reason of course. I am a team player, and sometimes I wonder if he knows because he never says a word and his attitude doesn't change as it did before. We hardly ever argue; we both state our piece, and if it's heated we walk away for a few moments and come back as one 97 percent of the time, before the sun goes down.

Ephesians 4:26 (KJV) clearly states, "be ye angry, and sin not: let not the sun go down upon your wrath." I get more upset with my husband than I do anyone else on the planet, and I had to learn that I wasn't a horrible person because I was angry, nor was he. However, the cursing and fighting, calling him everything except a child of God, had to stop. The Word is clear: do not sin in your anger. Colter and I have changed to fit the other's needs, and there is nothing we wouldn't do for each other. The Colter I am madly in love with today is not the same Colter I first married. The part of me that couldn't fall in love and wasn't bothered when people walked out the door has died. I am finally in a relationship that I will fight for, and if you don't believe it, try me :)

There is no better partner for me, and in him I have all that I need to live a long life of happiness. He gets on my nerves, please don't get me wrong. I'm sure I drive him crazy at times too, but I still love him even when it hurts to love him. When every part of me wants to say FOOL LEAVE, there is still no one else I'd rather be with. God does all things well, and if I've learned anything on my Christian journey it's to trust

God no matter what it looks like.

The problem I had cheating on people, and how easy it was for me to view it as "just sex", is gone. My husband has taught me what it feels like to be trusted, and thirty years old and four relationships later, I've never felt this feeling, to be trusted that is, until right now. I'm not talking about trust like "I check your phone every day when you're not looking, so I trust you because I know everything you're talking about and who you're talking to." Before Colter, I was never with someone who didn't make a habit of going through my cell phone. I've never been with anyone who trusted me beyond what they could see, and for trusting me without a doubt I can't and won't fail him—especially when I don't deserve him in the first place and he is a true blessing.

I mean that. Colter P. Nielsen has the best of me, and it's because he truly loves me. I can't and won't disappoint my baby. He deserves the best I can give him for giving me the best of him. Colter is not perfect as none of us are, but I've never seen a person, man or woman, so ready and willing to change for the better of himself and us. Getting him to listen may be a battle, but when my husband listens, he listens with all of him and change comes effortlessly. Now he might need a reminder in a month or so, but one text is all it takes and he's back on point like a needle.

The first year of our marriage was rocky; the devil was working overtime. Today I know it's because we were going to be the power couple that we are now. No matter what, no matter who, my husband is first. I hold true to the vows I made to him, and his happiness means more to me than my own. We have not only grown as a family unit, our relationship with Christ has blossomed as well. My mom always says that God favors marriage, and I sure believe that today. I have to ask God at times if He is ignoring the rest of the world for us. From monetary things to changing my husband or me for the good of our marriage...DONE.

Of course, now we've learned how to pray in the will of God, and that still doesn't mean He always has to say yes. My husband and I don't always do things right, but we fight to live right and allow conviction from God if need be. We both have submitted fully to His will for our lives, whatever that may be. God blesses us more than I could have ever dreamed of, and I am constantly in awe of Him. I praise God for my husband and everything that we've been through together. We hold hands and fight the enemy and stay equipped with the Word of the living God.

I pray that if God elevates one, He elevates the other and that we are always on the same accord. Matthew 12:25b (KJV) says, "and every city or house divided against itself shall not stand." I pray that if it ever comes to things of importance that we just can't agree on, God will take the wheel and convict one and humble the other according to His perfect will.

Early in our marriage submission was hard for me, but now I trust God and the God in my husband to lead the way. Ephesians 5:22 (KJV) says, "Wives, submit yourselves unto your own husbands, as unto the Lord." I about lost my mind when Pastor Frazier introduced this to us in premarital counseling. No way was I going to give him, or any him, that kind of authority over me. Then my pastor brought up a very good point. Pastor said that a husband who loves his wife won't treat her like "less than," and a few verses later (5:25) Paul says, "Husbands, love your wives, even as Christ also loved the church, and gave himself for it." If you love someone enough that you'd die for them, surely you wouldn't treat them like the scum of the earth.

I prayed and asked God to give me a heart of submission and allow me to fully trust my husband to lead our family, and to keep my husband following Him. God sure does answer prayer, even the ones you forget you've prayed. Today, my husband makes all the decisions in our house. Though I give my opinion and he always asks, the decision is ultimately his and I trust him fully. If God called my husband home now, I wouldn't know how to get to the money to pay a gas bill or anything else ending with the word *bill*. Having been someone who took care of most things in the relationship, it feels mighty good. I don't see a bill, I don't make financial decisions, but when I flip a switch the lights come on. When my car gets on E, in some mysterious way it goes back to F. If I am sick, I can take off work and the bills are still going to get paid. I can't explain how good that feels seeing as how I've always had to have an answer for everyone else.

I'm not boasting, and forgive me if you take it that way, but I hope every woman reading this book knows she deserves all this and then some. I felt unworthy for so long. I knew I didn't deserve all this, and before God changed my heart I didn't. Today, Colter is mine and no one deserves him more than me, and you can take that to the bank.

I recently got a speeding ticket, and when I picked up my phone I was about to call my godfather. Then I laughed to myself as I thought, *Oh no, this time my husband gets the honor*. God gave me Colter P. Nielsen, and I find it a privilege to call him husband. Thank you for making my heart beat, baby. I've been living, but now with you and God I am alive.

What About My Friends?

If I could have a job where I just got to meet new people and love on them, helping them tackle different obstacles, I'd be at work seven days a week an hour before everyone else. I have a genuine passion for people and a heart of compassion and understanding. Everyone has a story, and I wish I could get to know them all. I've learned so many lessons in my three-year walk with Christ. Things continue to fall off of me daily and be revealed to me daily. Almost everything was a smooth and easy transition, but not being able to keep all my friends (in my daily life) was and still is rough.

God knows us, and He definitely knows Shay, and He knew this was going to be my battle! Now before I start, let me tell you that 2 Corinthians 6:14 (GNT) says, "Do not try to work together as equals with unbelievers, for it cannot be done. How can right and wrong be partners? How can light and darkness live together?" If I am a thief and you are not, why would you want to be around me every day? One day I will be caught and you will be an accessory to the crime! You will never be able to convince anyone that you were with this thief all the time and didn't know she was stealing. You never enjoyed anything she stole? And you never thought for one second that you should not be around her or you'd get in trouble yourself?

The Bible also says 1 Corinthians 15:33 (GNT), "Do not be fooled. Bad companions ruin good character." That's the Word of God, not my words. It wouldn't be too long before you were tempted to steal yourself, seeing how easy it is and how many times they've gotten away with it. I've never been around anyone every day of my life and their habits not rubbed off on me. I've even found myself talking like people without ever trying to. It just happens. But when I became a Christian I found myself getting on the defense even with God. I wasn't losing my friends without a fight! I had so many excuses as to why these scriptures didn't pertain to me.

After going through discipleship training, I thought, *I have to be praying for five people so I need to be calling and checking up on them...we have to stay tight!* After I realized you can pray for someone without them being in your inner circle, I came up with another excuse. *How can I be a light to them if they are not around me?* Then when I realized that talking to some of my friends was like turning on rap music as much rebuking as I had to do, I needed another excuse. Trust me, there's a difference between a reason and an excuse.

God wants me to love everyone and show them His love. That means not turning my back on them; ergo I had to stay close to these people right? My mom gave me scriptures all the time to reference, but I already knew my friends would change, had to change. If my inner circle didn't change, could I truly say that I had? Living fully for Christ meant that my desires should change, what I liked and disliked should change, and who I cling to should change.

My mom prayed all the time that God would send me a young lady who was on fire for Him like I am so we could help each other grow. I can't tell you I prayed that prayer with her because I was happy with the friends I had. But God does all things well. Before I got saved, one of my close friends at the time got saved. Seeing how excited she was about

Jesus really put a fire under my butt. I knew her before she came to Christ, and she was changing for real. There's something about when you know a person previously and KNOW who they are now, and the two are totally opposite of one another. How can you not believe what is apparent and right in your face?

Her name is Chevalya Martin-Barr and I wanted whatever was happening to her to happen to me. Chevalya, whom we call Cha-Cha, was reading her Bible, going to church, and ministering to me without ever knowing she was doing so. With God pulling on my heart, it was perfect timing. We would sit on the phone for hours talking about God, calling seasoned believers asking them to break down scriptures for us. It was awesome! I also met another girl who was a member of a church I loved to visit. This young lady had a sense of humor that kept me laughing, and she listened to and laughed at my brutal honesty, never getting angry. Accepting the truth in its rare form, no sugar on it, is magnetic for me.

She and I started to converse on the phone daily, and she came by the shop often and always brought goodies. She had already been in church for awhile, so I was excited because though she was much younger than I, I could learn a lot from her. Her heart was so big, she was ready and willing to do anything her friends needed, never being disgruntled about it.

Another girl God sent my way was the youth pastor at an area church and knew the Word up and down, backward and forward, and she became my friend. I was mesmerized by her knowledge of the Bible and how sold out she was—and so young! Where I'm from, the people who were saved in and out of church were older, so forgive my awe. Anything I said to her about the Word, she knew it before I said it, and I was totally floored and excited about getting to know her. Cha-Cha, Lacey, and CeCe, these are the three friends God gave me at the beginning of my relationship with Him.

What About My Friends?

I still talked to Tisha, Malena, and a few other people I love to no end, but only during my secular part of the day if that makes any sense. I needed to stay rooted and grounded in Christ and get a solid foundation with Him before I fed myself to the wolves. I fell early in my walk but I got back up. Proverbs 24:16 (KJV) says, "A just man falleth seven times, and riseth up again: but the wicked shall fall into mischief." But I fell and I fell hard, and besides my mom, I called these three girls every day and they prayed me through this.

Cha-Cha and I were in the same storm but played opposite characters. I can't say much about it, but I will say we were both diligent, we both fasted, we both wanted and needed a particular thing from God, but we were totally submitted to His will. She and I were in this together, but in the end Cha-Cha didn't get what she wanted and I did. I was prepared to accept God's will, but I made my requests known to Him.

Do you know what Cha-Cha did for me? She was happier than I was when I overcame my storm, while still in the middle of hers! Most of you don't know how much love it actually takes for someone to accomplish this, because most of us can't do this. I am going to single myself out here because no matter what is happening with me, I can always be happy for my friends. And if I am truly happy for you, OUR happiness will wipe my sadness away. You can tell if someone has truly been praying for you by how much praise they have and how happy they are when you come out victorious.

Cha-Cha floored me. Not only did this girl praise and hallelujah until her heart couldn't stand anymore, she found peace and joy through her storm from my victory. Cha-Cha had done everything God said and was left with what looked like the extremely short end of the stick. Yet she was genuinely so happy for me, it made me feel bad. She looked at me with the biggest smile, a smile I hadn't seen on her face for the past year she had been going through. Cha-Cha smiled from her heart again! I will always cherish (*Cherysh*) that moment: No pun intended Cha!Lacey showed me how to serve and bend over backwards for people you love, even when you don't feel like it. That is something I struggle with, as I don't bother anyone except my husband, my godfather, and my mom, so I expect everyone to leave me alone. I learned from watching Lacey do anything and everything for people she cared about that this was a different expression of love—one I lacked in fully. However, we started to talk less and less about Christ and more and more about other people. I found myself sitting on the phone gossiping, for no reason other than having something to talk about. I could live my whole life not concerned about anyone else's business, good or bad, unless they invited me in. So why could we not get on the phone and talk about anything besides other people, negatively?

Over time I realized our friendship was not headed in the right direction and we had to throw in the towel. We started on the right path and somewhere along the way signals got crossed. We eventually just stopped talking, and though I miss her dearly, it was for the best. I don't want myself or her doing anything that not only doesn't give God glory but is sinful and makes Him angry. Gossip is an easy thing to fall into; even Proverbs speaks of how tasty it is. Gossip is not something I've ever struggled with before, and it's not something I want to pick up this late in life.

CeCe and I knew of each other when we were in the world, but we didn't know each other. We shared a bit of the same testimony, and when I found out she too was sold out to Christ, I was happy for her. We conversed often about Christ and how He delivered us. I could merely mention a scripture I was thinking of or wanted to study and she would quote it before I could finish my sentence! I loved it, she was on fire. We would sing gospel songs on the phone together, just listening to each other, never getting bored or hanging up.

I don't have the number of friends I used to have, but God gives me more love than any group of friends combined ever could. I thought I'd be saddened by the loss of people in my life, but missing people is completely different when God is happy because of it. Tisha is still my best friend, as my definition of a best friend is someone who can forgive you without a bruise. Tisha has earned that position in my life and giving that title to everyone would make everything she went through with me seem cheap. Tisha tells me every chance she gets how proud of me she is. It excites me when people who knew me most know that I am different. If He did it for me, He will do it for you!

When I joined Ebenezer Baptist Church, as warm as it was, I had a lot of insecurities that kept me in a shell. I was always afraid I wouldn't measure up to the women around me. My mom would always tell me who I would get along with, but I was too afraid. There was this one girl, Tierra Roberson, who came to my job one day and we had the best conversation. We kept in touch after that, and she was as down-to-earth and uplifting as anyone could be. I had just lost a few friends so I was welcomed Tierra in my life with open arms; not trying to replace anyone, but I love people. I had also prayed and asked God to give me the friends He wanted me to have, so I was excited! Tierra would always call me, text me, check on me...she was so warm. She never cursed, she wasn't a clubber, she was just sweet and loved her some Jesus.

When I was a nervous wreck, about to get married, she said, "Can we pray?" It was her prayers that calmed me and gave me peace. She prayed for me at my job when she could tell something was wrong with me. And everyone I worked with called her a church girl. Do you know what that said? Tierra's light shined in a place that I couldn't make my own light shine. I admired that. Tierra was young, and Christ was in charge of her life FOR REAL. She was the first person I gave my testimony to, and I remember the day we both sat at my job wiping tears. She said, "Shay, your testimony is going to deliver some people." God also used Tierra as the first person to confirm that I should write this book. Tierra is my little sister in Christ, but she is also my dear friend.

Brandi-B, you knew I was coming after you next right? How do I explain this girl? Selfless, matchless, invaluable, always the brain behind the project—that is Brandi-Berry Fulton. Brandi and I ran circles around each other when we were in the world. She and I hung around the same people, went the same places, yet somehow we never occupied the same space at the same time. I believe fully that God didn't want Brandi and I to taint our relationship in anyway so that we could arrive right where are! Brandi is now the kind of friend to me, that I was to others and I don't know how to receive it. I feel like I owe Brandi my life and our journey just begun. Guess I will be forever indebted to Brandi, she and Rod are those people whose worth can never be measured or fully repaid, but I won't stop in my efforts to show my gratitude.Brandi named this book before we knew I was even going to write a book. We were emailing each other back and forth, and I said, "My test is my testimony." She emailed me back saying something along the lines of "and my mess is my message!" When I first felt God tell me to write this book I didn't put thought into a title. When Brandi said that to me I knew that was the title and I've never changed it or even thought of another one. Brandi is saved, sanctified, and filled with the Holy Ghost. She walks and talks Jesus and is who she is 100% of the time. She's one of those people that you love or hate, and being that her honesty is what most people don't like about her, by now you know I am sold!

At only thirty years of age, she is the first lady of a church, where her husband, Andre Fulton, is the pastor. Brandi is a full-time wife and mother, she's in college getting her doctorate, she teaches Bible study every Tuesday night, and she is the owner/operator of an online accessory store, www.kompleteme.com, which I highly recommend to all the ladies for affordable fashion accessories. Tell me this diva is not one to watch and learn from. Not only does she have her own full-time life, but she makes time for everyone else's. I honestly don't know how she does it, but I plan to learn.

When Brandi and I started to open up to one another I told her I was in the process of fixing my credit. I explained to her that it wasn't very much debt on my report and all of it was from 2004 and earlier. Brandi stopped me mid sentence and said, "Don't you pay anybody! Those debts are over seven years old they have to take them off!" Brandi emailed me three formal well written letters (I couldn't believe someone I knew could orchestrate something like this) to send to the debt collectors and credit agencies and I stand here today completely debt free. The only money my husband and I ever spent was on stamps and sending certified mail! Brandi is brilliant and uses her talents and gifts to help not just herself, anyone she can. I am grateful to have her in my corner and I consider it a blessing to call her friend. Had I stayed in my own way and not let God move how He wanted to, where would I be, and whose friend would I be? Everyone in my inner circle now I am equally yoked with. I also have a brother in Christ that God gave me, Reginald Hardy, aka Poppa. People think we are real brother and sister and we are; depends on what you're definition of real is. I thank God for him, and appreciate all the joy and smiles that knowing him has added to my life. I actually met Chay through Reggie, as they are best friends. God took our awesome threesome and turned it completely around, saving us all from a burning hell.

Reggie is not the man he used to be, and I know that for a fact. I've seen his transformation with my own eyes. I thank God for his beloved wife, Devion Hardy. I give her and the God in her all the credit for my brother's drastic change. I don't know what kind of woman it takes to make a man like that fully submit to God and her, but I thank God for her being a light. Devion needs to be writing a book; she can teach us all something because Reggie was as much of a handful as any man. But when he started dating Devion, they had been friends for five-plus years, and he was totally different with her than he was with anyone else. When Reggie told me he was going to ask Devion to marry him at their church during a midweek service, I said I wouldn't miss it for the world, and I was right there!

He told me on the way to church the evening of the proposal, "She's the one, sis," and I knew he was serious. The change in him said that alone, even if he never said it from his mouth! When you know and love people, they don't have to say a word. God has given me friends that seek and love Him first, and we encourage and build each other up. My prayer now is that none of us is ever weak at the same time. If I am weak, I pray my friends are at the strongest point in their walk and willing to minister to me, and I surely will do the same for them. I pray I always tell them, and they always tell me, the truth in love. All these young ladies, and Reggie, seek and love truth and growth, and I couldn't call them friend if they didn't.

Though allowing God to build my friendships was hard, it was easy! God made sure it didn't have to come down to me calling people and saying "we can't be friends anymore." My mom can do that. Brandi can do that. Dee-Dee and Andrea can do that. But I can't do that, and I'm thankful to God that He didn't make me. Things and friends that weren't supposed to be have gradually faded away almost without my noticing. I thank God for changing my desires according to His will. Some things I used to do disgust me so much that I can no longer do them. Some people may not have understood my transformation and judged it as trying too hard or being fake. But God gave me a group of friends He had already delivered or was about to deliver, and my relationships with them have not hindered me in Christ but rather helped me to blossom, as God would see fit.

I hope I am the same motivation and influence for my friends that they are for me. I can't stress enough that God delivers us, not we ourselves. Now that God has delivered me, I feel the difference. There are problems I just don't have anymore. If you want it done right, whatever it is, allow God to do it. You won't have to go behind Him and check His work, trust me on this!

Alter Ego

I learned two things after the vision from God; that "no weapon formed against me shall prosper", (Isaiah 54:17) and also that "we wrestle not against flesh and blood", (Ephesians 6:12). It is not a surprise that I have heard both of those statements many of times, but once I *knew* these things like I know today is Sunday, there was no stopping me. As with many of us, there are two sides to who we are, some call this bipolar others call it an alter ego. My two different personalities are night and day, in fact those I love and myself named my alter ego, Shawn.

My nieces and nephews have heard so many stories about Shawn, if someone messes with them they threaten people by saying they will call Aunt Shawn. Combine a deep voice (something I mastered well over the phone) with the aggressive, protective part of me and you have my alter ego Shawn. I don't think anyone hated to see Shawn coming more than me, because I was always left feeling bad for Shawn's careless, raging, behavior. Call me strange and judge me how you will, but if there was no Shawn, I'd probably be back in the world right now. The enemy *could* have lots of weapons to use against me, and if I had no fight in me, those weapons just might prosper. I've never lost a fight before, and I won't lose one now; and if I could fight not knowing what could have happened, you can guarantee that I am ready for a battle that I am sure to win! When I tell my husband and friends that I am about to go to war with the enemy because I feel him lurking, I put my fist up; however my fist is not how the battle is won. Shawn puts on the full armor of God, and I war in the spirit.

I prepare myself daily for spiritual warfare by reading my bible before my feet touch the ground, but when the crafty devil sneaks his way in to me through people or circumstances, I turn on my war song, *I Told The Storm,* and I command that coward to MOVE, TODAY, RIGHT NOW! As the song says, "you don't have a choice in the matter, you have to cease", so glad that my father is all-powerful and when he says STOP it all stops. Even in the midst of what seems to be all hell breaking loose I am reminded that "nothing touches me that hasn't first passed through the hands of my Heavenly Father." My prayer before battle is always first for the forgiveness of my sins, especially those I may not be aware of. Then I tell God that if He's building character in me (by allowing what may look like a storm), give me the strength to get through whatever it may be because I know I will be better because of it. But if this is the devil, he's out of here, LEGGO (let's go)!

I make it my business to shut the devil down every chance I get as I have promised God in prayer that He can trust me on the infantry line to stand against the wiles of the devil- God knows if this is true. When I first started going to my church, every 5th Sunday we would wear army fatigue because we are soldiers for Christ on the battlefield (I wish we still wore it because I have never felt more like Christ's soldier). When I see my Pastor, I put my fist up and I hope he knows that it's not because I am warring against him, instead I am warring with him. This is what I was made for, what Shawn was made for. Now when my nieces and nephews call me Aunt Shawn, I smile and don't correct them at all. Aunt Shawn is right here fighting for you all every day, but not with her fist but on her knees. I have learned that the real victory is won on my knees.

We've all heard the term "come as you are" in reference to church and when God pulled on my heart, that's exactly what I did. For my entire life up until this point, the only time I "dressed up" was to go to the bars or nightclubs. Looking through new eyes, I now know my clothes weren't appropriate, but it was what I had. When God told me to get in church, He must have forgotten to provide me the church etiquette memo. I was an adult entertainer for years so my idea and the church's idea of "appropriate" were not exactly on the same page, or even in the same book for that matter. I am glad that my church family did not judge me based on my clothes.

I love my church family for many reasons, if I made a list it would go on and on; I appreciate each of them for loving me right where I was. Women in my church such as Vonda, MeMe, Tashi, Amber, Treva, Sheronda, Carmella, Quisha, Dawn, Shanae, to name a few of my peers, I am grateful for never looking at me with judgment but instead giving me the warmest welcome any visitor could ask for. The only eyes that ever starred down my cleavage or plumbers crack were the eyes of old faithful (my mommy), who had more than a right to check me in love. I truly didn't know better or have better but God will grow and mature us to what we need to be, but first we have to get in the door. Some "Christian" tactics push people out the door and not in the door; so glad that my Ebenezer church family not only pushed me in the door but loved me just as I was as I found my rightful place in Christ.

Easter 2012 I purchased my first women's suit and I must humbly say that I've never felt more beautiful. The new eyes that God has given me allowed me to see me the way He sees me and I thank Him for His gentleness when telling me none of my clothes worked. My entire wardrobe has changed and I now feel amazing in clothes that I would have once said were for my mom. I have given away *all* of my old wardrobe and everything in my closet can now be worn anywhere, while reverencing both

God and my husband. I thank God that the eyes that see me now will first see the God in me and nothing else (not my clothes or lack of clothes) will be a distraction.

Happy Birthday

The truth is not always painted in a beautiful package wrapped in pretty bows, but how will you know and grow if no one ever tells you? In retrospect the hard truth my mom and godfather leveled at me through the years was just what I needed. Whenever reality hit me in the face, I realized I had someone there the entire time, trying to block me from the blow. But God does all things well, and it was meant for me to go through everything I've gone through.

A lot of people wouldn't tell this story in rare form, as I myself walked away from the computer many times saying, "I can't do this." Ashamed, embarrassed, I didn't think I'd make it this far. I kept telling God, "Do You know how many people aren't even going to read for themselves, just listen to what someone else says and start terrible rumors about me?" Or "Some people will only read the 'mess,' but when the Bible scriptures come into play, they will stop reading, not knowing from where You've brought me. God, can I do this? Can I face this kind of persecution and deal with being judged to this level?"

I thank God for Brandi, from the basement of my heart. When I wanted to walk away, it was her words that put me back at the computer. I don't remember verbatim what Brandi said to me, but it was something along the lines of "we can't be ashamed of where we've been. The ability to freely speak of our pasts shows we are confident that God has forgiven and delivered us, but also allows others to be delivered through our testimony. Get back on that computer!"

Then there was another time we got busy moving, I was busy with work, and we just had a lot going on. I don't know if Brandi noticed that I talked about the book less, or if God simply used her, but a month went by and I hadn't touched the book at all. I started saying, "Lord, it must not be meant. You and I both know I'm ADD and can't concentrate on anything. I never stick to any one thing, why would I think I can write an entire book? Even if I could do it, I don't know if I could live with the persecution."

One day I got a card in the mail from Brandi and it read, "You Have What It Takes...Adversity can bring out the best in people, and that's certainly true of you...Your courage is an inspiration!" Then Brandi wrote, "Shay, you crossed my mind today, and I thought of all the lemons life has given you and I was inspired by the lemonade you made! Stay firm, faithful, and diligent as you complete your book! I can't wait to read it!" When God gives you friends, He gives you FRIENDS. I don't know if I would have finished this book had Brandi not encouraged and inspired me. This was not an easy project to start, BUT GOD BUT GOD BUT GOD!

To get back to my story, when Colter and I started dating one of the first things I asked him was, "Do you have kids and do you want kids?" I love my family, but if I could have it my way I wouldn't do the blended family situation, as some of us would if we had a choice. My son was in heaven; Colter had no children and he wanted at least two. We agreed fully in that aspect as we did many others.

After we were married, I had the baby blues from the moment I said "I do," so I thought holding my peace for three months was pretty good. Colter and I got married August 30, 2009, and I convinced him we should start trying by December 2009. We took a positive pregnancy test April 2010. I was happy, I was sad, I was scared, I was worried. Who would have thought one symbol on a test can get someone's emotions so fired up.

Because of the stillbirth of Chance and the placenta eruption that caused the stillbirth, I was high-risk from the very beginning. My doctor and his nurse were amazing throughout my whole pregnancy. From the moment I found out I was pregnant, I prayed and prayed and prayed. If the same thing were to happen to me twice, I'd never try to have another baby again in life! My mom prayed and told me not to worry every time I started to worry. My mom was out of town at a conference when the incident happened with my first pregnancy, and those of you who know my mom know she was mad that she couldn't get to her child in a crisis. She vowed that until her grandchild was here, she was not leaving the city.

My pastor prayed for the baby growing in my belly many Sundays and always asked me about the baby. My church family was praying for me, and I could feel it when I went to church, don't ask me how. I think you can just tell when people are praying for you by how they embrace you. They look at you to see if you're smiling again to know if God has worked it out, because prayer warriors know He will—they're just waiting until He does!

One particular month or so was really hard for me. I wasn't sleeping, I could hardly eat, I was worried and petrified. At church one of my mom's dear friends, I call her Aunt Jackie, walked up to me and gave me the warmest, most heartfelt hug. I didn't want to let go. She said, "Shay, I don't know what you're going through, but God put you in my spirit and in my heart last night, and I prayed for you. Whatever it is, God's got it, okay?" I wept and wept. So God used yet another vessel to deliver His message, I believe because of my disbelief.

Another time this beautiful well-dressed lady walked up to me and said, "God said to tell you that whatever it is, you have the victory over it." She hugged me and said, "I don't know what it is, but you don't have to fight the battle. God has already won it for you." It took everything in me not to fall in her arms and cry out to the Lord, "Thank You, thank You, thank You!"

After that I still worried, but it was more out of disbelief than true worry. As hard as it was to believe that two women who didn't know me well could tell me what God said to them about me, that fits so perfectly. How did they know it was God? I hear voices all the time. How do you decipher the difference? If I knew then what I know now! My heart is getting so full, my eyes so flooded with tears, that I might have to stop writing for tonight. To this very day that is how God speaks to me. Someone will confirm what I feel in my spirit or something I pray about privately, with me not having told a soul, even my husband. YOU CAN'T TELL ME IT'S NOT GOD!

I didn't see the well-dressed woman again for months. I didn't want to tell my mom that I was worried to this extent, so I didn't tell her for awhile, but I finally did. I told her I thought an angel came and spoke to me because I hadn't seen her again. My mom probably thought I was crazy, but she guessed who it was the very first time. She said, "That was probably Aretha, that's my girl!" My mom and I kept looking for her, and I would tell my mom every Sunday, "See, she's not here!"

The very first Sunday we saw her, my mom brought her to me and said, "Shalaunda, is this her?" I looked up and it was like seeing an angel. I grinned from ear to ear and wanted to grab her and give her a hug so big I could have jumped in her soul. I thank Aunt Jackie and Aunt Aretha for obeying God. Because of their obedience, I was given that precious peace that only God can give.

The rest of my pregnancy I walked by faith and not by sight. I embraced the peace that God had given me, feeling bad that He had to show Himself so I would calm down and believe that He would see me through. My "high-risk pregnancy" was as low-risk as any pregnancy could be. I did have to go to the hospital twice a week for awhile, and it was annoying, but I did it with a smile on my face, happy that I had a doctor who cared, was confident, and knew the appropriate steps to take.

My second pregnancy was the total opposite of the first one where I had complications from the very beginning. I think I had so many people praying for me, God was probably like, "I heard you all the first one hundred times, let me send some messengers to let Shay know that it's done!" I learned the power of prayer and the will of God through my worry. I believe fully that the prayers of others and my own, along with being in God's will, gave me total peace and victory. Matthew 18:19 (GNT) says, "And I tell you more: whenever two of you on earth agree about anything you pray for, it will be done for you by my father in heaven." And 1 John 5:14-15 says, "And this is the confidence we have in Him, that, if we ask anything according to His will, he heareth us: And if we know that he hear us, whatsoever we ask, we know that we have the petitions that we desired of Him."

I believe I had a multitude of people praying, not wanting me to face the same disaster. I could tell by the look on some people's faces that they worried about me and were trying to read me to see if I was worried, and at first I was. Philippians 4:6-7 says, "Be anxious for nothing; but in everything by prayer and supplication with thanksgiving let your requests be made known unto God. And the peace of God that surpasses all understanding shall keep your hearts and minds through Christ Jesus." I know I am so unworthy of this kind of peace, and to be honest, of all the inspirational words it was my least favorite. But now peace of mind is EVERYTHING! I thank God for His peace when I know I don't deserve it. Today, because of God's peace, I am unmovable.

I came to a point where I could say with confidence, "Oh, nothing is going to happen to this baby. *She* will arrive on time, perfectly safe and normal." I heard a preacher online once say, "When we ask God, we ask at a C-, and God is a God of an A+." That sure proved true to me because not only did our 7lb, 6oz bundle of joy arrive safely, I never had one complication. Not one emergency situation. Nothing that ever worried my doctor or me. THANK YOU, JESUS!

If God were to say, "Shay, I have to attend to another one of My children that needs me as you once did; I have done all I can for you, I love you!" I'd be fine for the rest of my life for what He has already done. I could spend the rest of my life saying thank you and it still wouldn't be enough. God has blessed me beyond my wildest dreams, and my heart overflows with gratefulness. I will forever trust Him.

My due date for this pregnancy was December 14, 2010, but because I was getting a C-section, my doctor scheduled me for December 8, about a week before my due date. My husband's birthday is December 6, so as we were writing the date in, I asked, "Can we do it a couple days before that on Monday, which would be December 6?" My doctor said, "Sure, I don't see why not," and my husband's birthday was stolen! On December 6, 2010, at 8:33 a.m., our beautiful daughter came into this world as healthy as any newborn can be: Happy Birthday Hubby! I thought I knew love, but when I met my daughter for the first time, love had a whole new meaning. Here's this precious baby so trusting and depending on her father and me for everything.

I prayed the same prayer my mom said she prayed over her children when they were born. I said, "Dear God, give me everything I need to raise this baby right. Give me discernment to respond to her needs, even when she doesn't know she needs it yet. Today and for the rest of my life, Lord, I need You more than ever. God, You trusted me with her and I know that means I can do it, even when it may look like I can't. Every child is different, so help me to learn my baby and raise her Your way together with You, my husband, and her grandparents, amen."

I was finally a mother, and this was the only time I've ever been proud of myself. I knew instantly when I held my baby that I was giving her my everything. She had changed me forever. I knew instantly that, unlike everything else in my life, I would not fail her or give up on her. Every decision I make in my life now, be it the company I keep or when I go to the store, is predicated on her. My life revolves around Chelyn, she doesn't revolve around mine.

My purpose in life now is to make sure she is taught everything she needs to be taught and has all the things she needs so that her future is as bright as it can be. It didn't take me ten years to feel this way, it happened the day we met. I couldn't believe I was holding my daughter when I first held her, WOW! As I looked at her, I just thanked God. Although when they held this baby up so I could see her, I wondered where my child was! How funny is it that my very African American behind just delivered a red-haired, blue-eyed baby girl? My first statement when I saw her was "thank You, Jesus," and the second was "is she albino?"

I stated earlier that black men just didn't like my physique and diverse frame of mind right? I always sort of knew, but my search for love ended with my tall, dark, and handsome German husband! I love that my baby and I are culturally different; we've never had any issues because of it. Our home is filled with laughter and lots of love, and the white baby that you see me with is mine! I've had people ask me everywhere if she is my daughter. I don't get upset or offended at all. Biracial children, mixed with black, are usually more black than anything. Until our baby girl, I'd never seen black and white children who were more white, but now we see it everywhere. My husband and I always say, "Look, baby, there's our daughter or our future son" as we both hope for a healthy baby boy in the near future.

Happy Birthday

Though my pregnancy with Chance ended tragically, I can now see God all over it. My son would have grown up with two moms, and maybe that would have had some bad effects once I decided to get saved. I'm not saying he needed to die for that, but everything isn't for everyone. What one person can survive another one can't. Chance obviously wasn't a fighter, and for the life I was about to bring him into he needed boxing gloves on. You just never know what God is sheltering us from. And at the end of the day, I know my baby is in heaven—there are no ifs, ands, or buts about it. I find more peace than ever knowing he is with God almighty. Please don't be sad for me; God does all things well and I am at total peace. I can talk about Chance and share the testimony with anyone it might encourage.

One thing I think both my husband and I learned through my worry and stress is the power of fasting and prayer. We always listened to our pastor preach about the power of fasting and prayer but thought it was for people in charge, not us. Once I learned that fasting was God's gift to all of us, I couldn't wait to see what it was all about. I started to ask God for small things through fasting and prayer, and I was amazed at how my fast produced everything I asked for. EVERYTHING! There was a point in time where I felt like I had magic, and if I wanted all the stop signs to turn blue, they would.

Now I know that is farfetched, but God was giving me everything I asked Him for IN SECRET. I remember being specific about this particular car I wanted, and when my husband and I started car shopping, it seemed too expensive, so I started shopping for other cars. You better ask somebody about the God I serve. In the garage is the car that I wanted from the very beginning—the car that my husband and I deemed too expensive. Not only did we get the car I wanted, we paid the price my husband wanted!

I also went on a fast about my job. Not only was the environment no place for a Christian to be every day, my brother and I did end up changing a lot when God changed us, but with so many ghetto "tattoo shops and parties" showing up around us, our shop was getting slow. I was worried, though I didn't let anyone know the extent of my fear. Our home needs two incomes. My husband could keep us afloat if need be, don't get me wrong, but I like to live comfortably! With no college education or experience doing anything other than tattooing and piercing, where would I work with any significant amount of income? I needed God to take the wheel, so I tried fasting again.

A girl who worked at another one of our shops had an RN degree, and she'd been looking for a nursing job for over a year with no results. This shop, Freaks on Broadway, was a completely different playing field than the shop I was currently at, Freaks on Troost. My godfather said that maybe I could go to Broadway if the girl found a job, but she had been looking to no avail for awhile. What did I do? I went on a fast. Though I wanted to go to Broadway after Rod convinced me, ultimately I wanted God's will for my life. If He was telling me that my career wasn't giving Him glory, I could accept that, but just show me where I am to go!

I had learned by this time to pray in the will of God, so I wasn't going to pray, "Lord, please get me to Broadway" if Broadway wasn't what He had for Shay. I kid you not, three weeks after going on this fast, the young lady found a job and I had a full-time schedule at the Broadway shop! Do you see why I felt like I could do magic? The favor of God has always been on my life, and you can't begin to grasp what my heart feels unless you've been here. I look at everyone else around me, like, *God, they haven't disgraced You the way I have. Why do You continue to answer my prayers and sometimes seem as if You ignore everyone else's?* I told God straight up it makes me feel bad. *If anyone doesn't deserve Your love and kindness, it's me!*

I've never felt true forgiveness until God forgave me. It feels like He doesn't remember a thing I have done! Before I pray I remind Him, "God, I know I have spit in Your face over and over, and I can't believe I can fix my mouth to ask You this...." Sometimes my guilt stops me from praying. God has let me know over and over again that He has COMPLETELY forgiven me and I am a new creature. Thank You, Jesus!

My husband and I definitely hope to have one more baby and call our family complete. We also accept God's will, and if that means no more children, we can live with that too. We are at a point in our lives where God is in total control and life has never felt better. To know that you can rest safely in the passenger seat and let God drive, not having a worry at all, is awesome.

Back in October 2011 we found out we were pregnant again, but it was an ectopic pregnancy and had to be surgically removed. I was told I could lose my Fallopian tube as well. My fear only lasted for a moment as I realized I should be thanking God my tube didn't rupture, causing me to bleed to death. Yet again God was saving me from something else. I remember waking up from surgery, and the first face I saw was my pastor's—I couldn't have felt safer. Knowing that he was there praying gave me peace that nothing but what God wanted to happen would happen to me. I did end up losing my tube, which means a possibility that becoming pregnant will be harder, but after reading this far, surely you know that I know THERE IS NOTHING TOO HARD OR TOO BIG FOR GOD! If it's in His will, it *will* be. At this point in my life, I sit back and watch God work!

I Came For Deliverance

I have had several concerns about living a righteous life, however what I learned from being a living testimony is that even what seems to be my biggest problems are small to an all powerful God. So many put on a façade for others as they race to hold the title of "the best Christian" and I can honestly say that has never been me. I just had a deep and burning desire to be as fulfilled in God, as I was in the world. Some people say that while in the world they were miserable and their previous life of sin was a punishment, but I won't dare tell that lie, I had fun and a lot of it. Seriously why would you or I be miserable fulfilling the desires of our flesh- what comes natural to us? The desires of our flesh are things God deems as "sin" and sin separates us from the communion of God while we are living but the consequences can be far greater as sin can also separate us from God eternally. But if you don't believe or at least know this, why would sin make you miserable?

I've heard a sermon or two about the importance of renewing our minds, but until mine was renewed, I didn't understand the significance. Without a renewed mind, we as believers are just actors on stage mimicking the lives of other believers. Not only will our acts not be accepted by God, as the bible says, "this will take place when God judges people's secrets through Jesus Christ" (Romans 2:16). My logic tells me that it is pure torture, at least mentally to be in a place you don't desire to be. There cannot be happiness or joy in creating a façade where you are pretending to be happy. Everything I've done in my life was because I wanted to do it and living for God was not going to be any different. I thank God that though I didn't know the importance of praying, "Lord give me a renewed mind and heart", He did, and renewed I am.

I don't call it a bad thing that I wanted to please God instantaneously, so ShaLaunda delivered Shay. I called it then "self deliverance"; ShaLaunda did what was necessary with the weapons that God had equipped her with to push Shay to the next level. Guess what though, at first I was holier than thou; I could picture me in Heaven walking on the streets of gold! I was going to church every Sunday, reading the bible everyday and could not for the life of me understand why I was NOT *different*. I felt bad for my secret thoughts and I soon learned that the heavy feeling I felt was conviction. Conviction is that feeling we need in order to invite change. Tired of feeling convicted and believing that my "magic moment" must be *really* far away, I made up in my mind that self-deliverance must be how everyone who was saved did it and eventually good habits are created.

I refrained from (hence the word refrained) secular music, profanity, gossiping and anything else sinful. I turned my nose up to anyone that wasn't as holy as I, or who openly defiled *my* God. I'd look at people with judgment thinking, "How can you be so naïve, God doesn't like ugly so He sure doesn't like you!" In my eyes I was "God's pet", I was the only one worthy. I'm sure it will come as to no surprise to some of you that suddenly, the job of self deliverance was too much work and I couldn't hold on to the recent acting job that I wasn't getting paid for.

One of my favorite songs is by Lyfe Jennings, *26 years & 17 days*. Powerful song, if you have never heard it listen (after you finish reading the book of course). As a matter of fact purchase it on iTunes. In verse one Lyfe talks about how he is at his grandmother's house looking for God, only God isn't where his Grandma said He would be and he needed God at that moment. That was how I was feeling when my idea of deliverance failed, and I thought for sure that God deemed me unworthy because of everything I'd done in my life. My mom assured me that God wanted to show me who He was and surely everything I needed and wanted to be delivered from would take a lot longer than 90 days! We chuckled and as always I trust my mom, so I changed my prayer to God teach me how to be still and wait on you.

Recently, well into writing this book, I heard Bishop T.D. Jakes say in a sermon, "God can't deliver you from temptation, and it still be temptation." If you've ever been delivered from anything, I'm sure that statement was just as profound for you. Remember the first thing God delivered me from was homosexuality and I was certain that of all the things I would struggle with, women would be the hardest to overcome. There were times when I was fully engaged in my life of sin that I'd think about how I wanted to make my mom and grandparents proud and live right, but I knew that meant giving up women and that was something I didn't believe I could ever do. Yet it happened and I have not struggled or been tempted since my deliverance, a woman cannot move or motivate me at all in the sexual sense anymore. So I, ShaLaunda knew without a doubt what it felt like to be delivered by God. God's deliverance means you cannot be tempted by that thing, you are totally free and you if go back it was your choice (free will).

New Years Eve 2009, my husband and I went to church; talk about a new normal. At that point, I'd been a cigarette smoker for ten years and quitting was no concern of mine; not anytime in my near future anyway. I had already asked my Pastor how God felt about my cigarette habit and after my Pastor assured me that cigarettes won't *send* me to Heaven or hell, only get me where ever I am going faster, I was perfectly comfortable smoking cigarettes and being a follower of Christ. During the New Years church service, my Pastor told the congregation that if anyone had anything they needed to leave in 2009; to come to the altar, lay it down, and leave it there. A quick self-check allowed me to immediately see there were numerous things I needed to leave in 2009, but afraid it would be another bout with "self- deliverance" I remained seated.

I've never been one to talk to myself, so all jokes to the side, I was certain this day that if I have never needed a psychiatric evaluation, I now needed one as soon as possible. *Something* kept telling me to go to the altar and leave cigarettes; the cigarettes I was totally comfortable with smoking, the cigarettes that I couldn't wait to smoke when church was over or we left which ever came first. I hushed the noise in my head and for the life of me I couldn't understand two things; why did I change my mind about smoking all at once and why am I talking to myself? Then I thought maybe it is not I who was talking, scared to take the chance of the voice possibly being God, I got up and made the walk to the altar where I left the cigarettes.

I don't know for sure if I expected anything to happen, or if it was the fear of God alone that motivated me to go to the altar, but I did know that obedience is better than sacrifice and not going wasn't worth the risk. My husband and I left church and in anticipation of smoking my next cigarette, I had it lit before we made it off church property. Floored, awed, shocked, amazed, whatever word I choose won't describe the amount of disbelief I was in! Ten years I smoked cigarettes and if they were ever this nasty or smelled this bad, smoking would have never been an option for me. I smiled ear to ear as I held back tears and threw what would be the last pack of cigarettes I have ever purchased, out the window.

December 2012 marks three years since I have been a non-smoker. Out of disbelief a few times I have attempted to smoke cigarettes and to my surprise they were still gross; when God delivers, He delivers. A ten-year addiction that most people struggle trying to kick was gone just like that because God said so! "God cannot deliver you from temptation, and it still be temptation!" My eyes were opening to how powerful deliverance from our Heavenly Father is and I began to live my life in anticipation of what would be wiped from me next. I turned my mind and heart fully toward God and focused on the prayer, *"remove anything from me that is not like You and will eternally separate me from You."* Most of the time I pray with my mouth open where my voice can be heard but sometimes I think the words and pray with my heart. My first prayer was change my heart and mind and one of the most jaw dropping events for me to date, is watching God answer prayers that I never open my mouth to speak aloud. God judges the heart of man; guess He listens to our prayers from there as well.

Stumbling upon a version of the bible, the Good News Translation also referred to as the GNT, was the best thing to happen to me since writing. It was a version that I could understand and I recommend to all new believers. Finding a version of the bible that you can relate to and that doesn't contradict the King James Version is important as a believer. My mom and Brandi do not study from the GNT, but my husband and I love it, it is all about personal preference. Just understand it has the same meaning as the King James Version. Knowing the word of God for yourself is your best defense against fighting and defeating the enemy. Nonetheless, once I discovered the GNT, I reread most of the things that I had already studied just because I was intrigued. Finally, I could hide the word of God in my heart.

I read the book of James repeatedly and each time became more convicted. "Words of thanksgiving and cursing pour out the same mouth. My friends, this should not happen" (James 3:10). My heart was heavy as I instantly realized that out of the same mouth I praised my Heavenly Father, I could paint the air in beautiful colors (in the words of my Pastor) and if you didn't recognize the tone of my voice, you'd assume I was a different person. I wept as my heart cried out to God, "forgive me Father, I didn't know." Conviction comes with humility, but with humility comes repentance; and as I cried and felt ashamed, God was changing me yet again. I've learned many things about God by submitting to Him and He has continually proven that my prayers are not falling on deaf ears. God is honor-bound by His word to hear our prayers, if we live in His will.

The very next day on my way to work, I browsed through my twelve disc changer looking for my cruising music for that day, and yet again, as many times on my Christian journey, I thought I had lost my mind. I remember thinking I was in the wrong car as I turned on my T.I. CD and the cursing completely perturbed me. My first thought was, "Shay stop faking, your Pastor is not in the car with you." I kept it playing thinking that maybe I would get into the groove of things but the words grew more vulgar and and I was turned off by the sound of what I use to call music. T.I. was out the CD player before my fifteen-minute commute to work was over; and if you know me, you know how I *use* to feel about T.I.

I'm a living witness; if you want God to show you, who He is, tell your heart to ask Him. "God can't deliver you from temptation, and it still be temptation."

Today, my music choice has changed completely and gospel music is my first and only *love*. During this era in my life, when God was shaping me, every sermon my Pastor preached ministered directly to me; and you can bet your last dollar that when I went to church that next Sunday, my Pastor preached about protecting our ear gates and eye gates because that is how sin enters our minds. Then I remembered a saying I heard years ago, "what the eyes see and the ears hear, the mind believes." If I wanted my mind to change, what I put in my mind had to change; ergo the entrances to my mind had to be protected. My secular music life is almost no more because I don't have the desire; it doesn't give me the fulfillment it once did. There is a spiritual war inside of us and the only way our spirit will have victory over our flesh, is if we feed our spirit more than we do our flesh. The next time you turn on your IPod or Pandora, (like a well adjusted person in the twenty-first century); ask yourself, "Who's being fed?"

My love for music was also fueled by my love to dance; and neither of my "hobbies" was as fulfilling in my living room as they were in a social atmosphere. My husband and I were in our 20's when we met so neither of us was wanted to give up our youth because we were saved; therefore we went to nightclubs and bars when we desired to get out the house. My husband and I were both confident that going to have a cocktail and dance couldn't make us any less saved. It didn't take 20/20 vision to see that the night clubs/bars were not the place for us because it almost always ended in some type of physical altercation. My mom explained that we have to know our enemy and it is crystal clear that this lifestyle is not for you two. My mom went on to say that maybe going out is ok for some people, but I'm sure it doesn't end in violence; and to whom much is given much is required- look how God is blessing y'all, and don't ruin your testimony!

Within two weeks of the conversation I had with my mom, two things happen: *don't ruin your testimony* played in my head over and over like a rerun of *The Cosby Show*, and a friend that had given me one of the most sincere I am proud of you speeches I'd ever heard, lost every marble in her brain and totally forgot who she was talking to. I realized that I had ruined my testimony with her in particular because my talk and walk contradicted one another. The friend that I am speaking of had witnessed me curse my husband from head to toe in a violent rage and attempt to fight anyone who tried to touch me; and that gave her comfort to say things to me that totally offended me. I realized that I could not even attempt to be upset with her but only myself. My husband and I together agreed that our mom was right and we made a commitment to one another and to God, to let go of our night life- we were tired of the humility we woke up too, having to face the fool we made of ourselves the night before. What God has done for me is nothing shy of amazing and I refuse to let anything taint His victory in my life.

When we pray, "Lord lead us not into temptation", let's remember not to take ourselves there. Clubs and bars bring out the worst in me, so I gave the desire to sing and dance the night away, to God and told Him to have His way. Today, I have no desire to go to a bar of any kind and as a matter of fact, the last time I was bamboozled into going to a nightclub, looking through my new eyes that God has given me, I can give you more than ten reasons why I will not and should not be there. I now sing in the choir at my church and take vocal lessons with Mrs. Mary Jane Williams, one of the most encouraging, inspiring women of God I have ever met I thank God for allowing me to cross her path. I am still no singer; but remember I just said I love to sing not that I can sing! God has also changed my dance to the holy dance and it's ten times more rewarding and fulfilling than just dancing and I haven't lost any of me; I'm just on a different team, the winning team.

With so many changes taking place in my life daily, you would think the state of shock was no longer a state for me, but the norm; but in fact I became more shocked as God has never been more evident in my life. I could no longer deny the voice of *something* in my head and the word coincidence is no longer in my vocabulary. When I first started on my Christian journey, I thought I had faith in God at least the size of a mustard seed, but in reality I wanted to have faith in God; I desired to have faith in God- and in turn my heart was opened to hear his voice and God made Himself known to me. I now see beyond whatever may be in front of me and I trust the voice of God. I've also learned how His voice speaks directly to me. Just as parents treat children different according to their individual needs; I believe fully that God our gracious merciful Father is the same way.

Shortly after God delivered me from my former love of the nightlife; it only made sense that the nightlife's cousin alcoholic beverages had to go. I did appreciate my "nightcaps", and I don't believe the nightcaps would have been so bad if they didn't become stronger, more frequent, and eventually turned into stress relievers. I began to have headaches, and having headaches is something I am no stranger to. This headache was unusual as it lingered around for a week and nothing gave me relief from this nightmare that resided physically in my head. After a few days of pain I began to pray; usually when I have headaches I only pray for the strength to get through but this time the Holy Spirit guided me in prayer. While praying I asked God if He didn't want me to drink, lift the tormenting headache from my body. I laid there in total awe because in less than twenty minutes after praying, I slept like a baby and as I rose the next morning, I felt better than I'd felt in a long time. I know I should have been certain that God didn't want me to drink and relieving my headache was my answer, but I was confused. I decided I'd pray for clarity. Maybe I was attempting to justify my desire to drink; nonetheless, it didn't make sense to me regardless.

Two days after God relived me from the headache, I was sick yet again; but nothing I hadn't had before, I simply called my doctor and he called in a prescription, no big deal. So annoyed with the infection before I left the pharmacy I opened the bag to take my first dose, and the first warning on the label I seen was "NO ALCOHOL!" Sure it was there with my name, address, and all the other formalities but these letters were huge and bold jumping off the bottle directly for me to see. God didn't want me to drink and I heard Him loud and clear. Of course Brandi knew what was going on so I had to send her a picture of the label so my jaw wasn't on the floor alone; Brandi and I live in constant awe of God and not only is she my prayer partner, she's my praise partner.

I continually praise and thank God for molding me to His image, and directing my life to line up with a life that will please Him. If God never tells me I can have another drink, I am absolutely fine with that, because when God told me not to drink, He had already taken the desire to drink. "God can't deliver you from temptation, and it still be temptation." My husband watched his wife go from a Crown on the rocks before bed about four or five nights a week, to not even being able to tolerate the smell of liquor. My husband gave me the "are you ok face" for about a month before he realized the magnitude of what God had done in His wife. "When God knows He is first in your life and He can't be moved, He will move on your behalf."

I can be passive aggressive and alcohol seemed to only intensify the *aggressive* and eliminate the *passive*. The result of me drinking alcohol is my anger that I thought I had control over, showed it had control over me. Throughout my 30 years of life I have always been both violent and angry. In an attempt to keep peace I found that I became extremely passive. One can only conceal how they truly feel for so long and as unfortunate as it is when I decided to stop concealing how I feel my anger was unleashed on the people I love the most. I would have a fit and explode on the ones I love without them even having knowledge of why. How unfair to them, here I am exploding and raging about things they never knew was a problem. I am certain if I had given them a chance, those who love you will do whatever it takes not to upset you if you set boundaries. Letting people know your boundaries, should never be offensive but received in love as a part of getting to know one another. I would find myself in fits of rage because I put myself in positions that I never gave my "offenders" inkling that they were committing offenses against me.

Of all the things I have been delivered from, who would have thought my anger would be what I struggle with? Conviction about my anger came one night after having a heart to heart with my husband and he shared with me the genuine concerns of his heart. I had to listen and digest as the man I love told me that he was afraid of what I could do when I get mad. My husband went on to say that I get so infuriated that he believed fully if he mentioned Jesus or even laid the bible in my face, it wouldn't do anything at all. For someone who feared, loved, and obeyed God as much as I do, this broke my heart to hear and I was ashamed of my behavior.

I lay in the bed that night convicted, as I was now face-to-face with my anger. The conviction was so painful that it led to unstoppable tears. My husband kneeled next to me and told me not to cry and gave me a firm but friendly reminder where God had brought me from and continue to trust that same God. I told God in prayer that if I was going to be delivered from being passive and angry, He was going to have to take my free will from me and take total control. Lord knows I live to please Him, but how do I change me?

I surrendered what needed to be changed in me to the Lord and I was totally honest with Him; I was scared to fail- scared to fail God, my Husband, and my daughter. My friend Brandi told Colter and I to do *The Love Dare* (a book of forty love dares for married couples based on the movie *Fireproof*), to help us face areas of weakness in our marriage, even "the best" marriage has some grey area. I didn't think about attempting the dare when Brandi told me about it, but the Holy Spirit dropped it my spirit when I needed it the most. The book didn't waste any time getting to the root of my problems- *Day 13, Love Fights Fair*. This day's dare entailed the best approach to heated situations and teaches how to fight clean. The dare for this day was to write down *we* boundaries and *me* boundaries; and as a rule of thumb either of us has the right to gently but directly enforce these rules if they were violated.

I put my head in my lap and opted to pass on this particular dare, as it gave us a choice to pass if we were not ready, I honestly wasn't ready. The next morning on our way to church, I had a vision from God and it was the first I'd ever had. In the vision it was relative to a first player video game, you know the one where you can only see your weapon? I stood in front of this huge fog of dark black smoke and I couldn't see anything; but somehow I knew that what was in front of me was the spirit of anger. Suddenly through the middle of the fog, it started to lighten and I could see through it. Standing on the other side with His arms wide open waiting on me to run to Him, was Jesus! In the vision, I channeled all the anger I could feel in my body, toward running through the fog into the arms of my Lord. As I fell in His arms, He hugged me and I felt Him say, "Well done!" I cried and cried before we ever made it to church that morning. My husband just rubbed my hand; he never asked what was wrong or right we have that connection. Our connection allows him to know when he sees tears, first assume gratefulness and praise not hurt or pain. I went home that day and wrote my "we" and "me" boundaries and told my husband, "We can do this, I'm ready!"

I now celebrate small victories understanding that it may not be one big pow, but a series of small pows, as God delivers me from my anger. I am not focused on the battle; I am here to win the war! Since God has given me the vision, I have celebrated five small victories and the last one wasn't small by any means, to God be the glory! Not only have I been calm in situations that would have normally sent me over the edge but one incident opened the door for me to minister the love of Jesus Christ, and I took full advantage! A stronghold is a victory the devil has over a certain area in your life; and I don't know about you but the only victories in ShaLaunda "Shay" Nielsen's life, will be celebrated by God and I. I'm so glad God gave me a new set of eyes to see these situations with and the knowledge on how to deal with them. If God brings me to it, He will bring me through it; a huge part of our defense against the enemy, is *believing* that.

Victorious

To God be the glory for all He has done, what He's doing, and what He is going to do! Who I am today is authentic. God has taken me out of my former life of sin and given me a new life in Him. I am forgiven, I am saved, and I am on my way to my destiny. The favor of God is upon my life, as undeserving as I am. I've watched God mold me into the woman I am today, the mother I am today, the daughter I am today, the wife I am today, the friend I am today, and the stranger I am to you today.

I'm not who I used to be, and I give God all the praise for taking control of my life. I hope that my life's story has encouraged change to a rebellious sinful mind, hope to a defeated praying mom, and introduced the love of God to those who may not know Him. Wherever you are on your walk through life, God can meet you right where you are if you accept Him and ask Him to come into your heart. All you have to do, all I did, was trust God and allow Him to have His way, and I was serious about it; God knows our hearts. We can't be fake with Him like we are with each other. We can't hide who we are from God, and I dare YOU to try Him today. You won't regret it! No matter how lost you think you are, no matter how much hope is gone, God is ready and waiting to restore it all.

Everything that the devil has taken is waiting on you in the safe arms of Jesus. I've aired out all my dirty laundry so that you reading this may say, "I'm not as bad as she was, and look at what God has done for her."

Or, "Okay, God, I may have taken my life a little further down the same road Shay was traveling, but she said You have room for me as well." No matter what it looks like, if you are alive there is nothing God can't and won't forgive. You have yet to feel forgiveness like God can give you, and none of us are worthy, but He offers it to us all freely.

Even while writing this book I've changed so much. I've ministered to myself as I pray, "God, give me the words to say, minister to Your people through my testimony." During two separate conversations with Brandi and another friend of mine whom Christ had recently called, the movie *The Passion of the Christ* was brought up. This was during Lent, and though we are not Catholic, my husband and I fast the forty days leading up to Easter Sunday. I took the movie popping up so frequently as a subliminal message, so I texted Colter immediately and told him we were going to watch *The Passion of the Christ* the Saturday before Easter.

I was so excited to watch, and not because I hadn't seen it before because I had, but I hadn't seen it since being saved. I was really stoked—not realizing that my relationship with Christ was about to undergo another facelift! My husband and I watched the DVD, and about an hour into the movie I had to stop it. To see the movie is one thing, but to see it when Christ is EVERYTHING to you, knowing that He suffered FOR YOU...my heart couldn't stand it. I wept and wept so much that if you'd walked into my house, you may have assumed my entire family had just been murdered. The tears were uncontrollable. To think also that if it were just Shay while she was on a stripper pole, if it were just Shay while she was snorting cocaine, if it were just Shay while she was running around fighting people because they "deserved it," He still would have suffered so severely. O God, forgive us, we KNOW NOT WHAT WE DO!

Though I didn't make it through the movie, something changed on the inside of me yet again. I realized the extent of what God did for me on crucifixion day. The picture was painted clear of what happened. Brandi told me that she tells her children, "Every time you disobey or act out in school, you re-nail Christ to the cross." Brandi's babies were bothered by this movie, wanting to beat up the bad men, bless their hearts. Her saying that to me ministered directly to me. I believe with my whole heart I was supposed to watch that movie when I watched it. I've said I was a protector right? Well, guess what? I love Jesus and I want to protect Him! I wanted to jump through that TV and kill somebody! And though Jesus doesn't need me to fight His battles, from that day forward I vowed to Christ that I will always fight on His team.

I said, "Lord, You may not need me to fight for You, but I will fight with You." I can stand here today and say with total confidence and certainty, "There's no turning back for me, for I will never be the same again!" God can count on me to stand firm on the infantry. I live my life daily thinking about what happened to Christ on that day, and it makes me want to FIGHT. When I was in the world I was a fighter, and in Christ I am nothing less. I fight to live right and I fight the devil every day. When I see that punk trying to attack my husband, me, and my family, I put on the full armor of God and go to war. I stand toe-to-toe with that clown and say, "What you got, I AM READY!" That coward backs down every time; he has nothing for my God! We win in the end. Get on the right side, family and friends!

Since that movie, my heart has been opened up to praise and worship in a totally different way. Songs that didn't move me before open my heart in a way I couldn't describe if I wanted to. On Easter Sunday the choir sang a song about Jesus going to Calvary to save a wretch like you and me. My heart was so full that tears streamed down my face. Everyone else probably already had this experience the first time they truly realized what Jesus did for them, so forgive me if you see me weeping it's my turn!

They did a skit at church that Easter Sunday and I couldn't even watch for crying too hard. I felt like such a crybaby. Keep me in your prayers because God is dealing with me and my ability to bury my feelings. God is revealing a weaker more vulnerable side of me, and my natural instinct is to hide it. With thirty years of practice, I am pretty good at it. But as a Christian, I don't want to bury my feelings, my praise, my worship from God or anyone else.

My husband and I have fallen in love with Jesus, and we don't just go see Jesus on Sunday mornings—He is everywhere we go! We are raising this precious daughter of ours in the fear of the Lord. Pastor, and my sweet first lady, you guys can trust that we are representing our house and your name well. I love you guys, and as long as God says the same, you will be my pastor and first lady until God calls one of us out of here! Thank you both for all that you do, because who you are pours all over our fellowship, and we are a blessed church because the head is the real deal!

I love my entire church family, and I can't wait to become active in ministry. Lord knows I'm not saying I need a ministry with a microphone and platform, because all duties are equally important and whatever God shall have me do, I will give my all. I've signed up to be on the cleaning committee at church, and I pray that I am devoted, committed, and always desire to clean God's house better than my own. And if God never calls to do anything else in ministry but clean, guess what? I am good at cleaning so I can get it done and well, and I have my hands full already with my first ministry. My Christian walk alone is my ministry. Being a wife is my ministry. And being a mother is my ministry. I will clean with great pride and a great spirit, knowing that I am giving God all the glory. My job cleaning is as important as any other in the sight of God, the only eyes that will judge Shay!

To my family, my peers, and my friends reading this book, if you try

God for yourself, you will find He is incapable of failing you. God can do anything but fail! My life was a mess. Hell was my destination, but God has forgiven me and given me all that I can ask for and more. When you are ready, when you feel God or "something" telling you to get your life in order, give God a try. You can't do it on your own. Give Him the same effort and energy you are giving your sinful life right now, and you will feel His presence! God will reveal Himself so true, so undeniable, but you have to do your part.

Our blessing and our curse is free will. If God pushed all the buttons and made us do what He wanted, what would our own hearts be needed for? But our part is the easy part. All we have to do is genuinely want Him, desire to change, and He will do the rest. If your heart is for real and you have just a little faith, the Bible says in Luke 17:6 (GNT), "...if you had faith as big as a mustard seed, you could say to this mulberry tree, pull yourself up by the roots and plant yourself in the sea, and it would obey you!"

Do you know how small a mustard seed is? God is asking so little of us to give us so much of Him! Don't worry about anything you may lose or gain, as God will work it all out in your favor and give you everything you need; and the things you don't need you won't miss, I promise you. If being rich means having everything you want, call me a billionaire! In Christ, I have everything I want, and I know how much it sucks to always want STUFF. I am freed from always wanting. It seemed like I was never satisfied and always unhappy because the minute I got something, I wanted something else. To never be satisfied is an awful feeling, and though it may seem like I had everything when I was in the world, I was always wanting something, therefore I was always unhappy.

Today I am totally satisfied, and there is NOTHING I want or need that I don't have. Try God; it's better on this side. I have everything that it "looked" like I had before, and I also have a head I can hold high. I live a life that pleases God, and I don't have to be embarrassed about anything.

To the mothers who are praying for their children the way my mom prayed for me, I declare that God will give you the desires of your heart if you live in His will. My mom is a living witness. Proverbs 10:24 (GNT) says, "The righteous will get what they want, but the wicked will get what they fear most." I am not a mom who has been up all night praying for a child, so I can't speak much about it, but I know what my mom did! I am evidence of what the prayers of the righteous produce. God is all you need to get your baby out of whatever it is; THERE IS NOTHING TOO BIG FOR GOD. But you can't be a mess yourself and demand God's favor.

My mom's testimony is powerful. I feel bad that she had to worry over me, but in God worry is not the same. Now when I worry, it's because I know what I deserve. Then the Holy Spirit reminds me that grace is unearned, underserved favor- and all traces of worry disappear. Once God's peace dwelled in my mom- unexplainable! That's why she's over fifty and is still knock-out gorgeous, her hair is still healthy, her face isn't sunken...we all know what people look like who don't sleep from worry! God does all things well.

As God and I wrap up this book with this final thought, I want to say yet again that the only thing stopping you is YOU; it is not God's will that any of us should parish. Seek God and everything else will fall into place according to His perfect will for your life. He does not have the same thing for everybody, so don't want what I have, or what Brandi has, or what Tierra has, but want what God has for you! Open your mind and your heart to accept His will. Know that you deserve death for your sins. Romans 6:23 (KJV) says, "for the wages of sin is death, but the gift of God is eternal life through Jesus Christ our Lord."

There is nothing God won't forgive you for as long as you are alive to ask. So if you are reading this, it's not too late. No matter what mess you're in, you too have a message. While writing this book, I started with so much shame and fear of judgment. There were so many times I didn't think I was going to make it through, but with my mom's encouragement, my husband's support and encouragement, Tierra's inspiration and soft-spoken heartfelt words, and Brandi's motivation, I got back up and said, "God, we can do this!"

When Brandi sent me that card, I prayed, and after I prayed I was released from my shame. The heavy burden I carried of what people would say about me, my husband, my daughter, or my mom was lifted. I thank God for His forgiveness because for the shame to be gone, I was first forgiven, and I've accepted His forgiveness (knowing how unworthy I am). THANK YOU, JESUS, for I am no longer a prisoner of shame, I am released from guilt, and *my mess has become my message!* God bless!

CPSIA information can be obtained at www.ICGtesting.com
Printed in the USA
LVOW071245111012

302393LV00001B/17/P